HALLOWING THE TIME

GEOFFREY PRESTON O.P.

HALLOWING THE TIME

*Meditations
on the cycle of the
Christian liturgy*

Texts
prepared by
Aidan Nichols O.P.

PAULIST PRESS
New York/Ramsey

First published in Great Britain in 1980
by Darton, Longman & Todd Ltd
89 Lillie Road
London SW6 1UD

©The English Province of the Order of Preachers 1980

Published in the U.S.A. in 1980
by Paulist Press

Editorial Office:
1865 Broadway
New York, New York
10023

Business Office:
545 Island Rd.
Ramsey, New Jersey
07446

Library of Congress
Catalogue Card Number:
80-82253

ISBN:
0-8091-2339-8

Printed and bound in the United States of America

Contents

Preface

Father Geoffrey Preston's first posthumous collection of spiritual conferences, *God's Way to Be Man* (Darton, Longman and Todd, London 1978), has been found helpful and inspirational by so many people that I have felt not only warranted but *obliged* to put together a second collection, offered in this book as *Hallowing the Time*. Although the texts gathered together here can speak for themselves, some acquaintance of a more personal kind with their author highlights and explains, I think, the notes of urgency and poignancy which the reader may pick up in them from time to time. It was because of this distinctive personal voice that it seemed right to preface *God's Way to be Man* with a biographical sketch; and in this further collection I take the opportunity, or the liberty, of contributing a more individual and less 'identikit' image of the Christian man whose words they were. I shall base it on my own most enduring impression from the years I knew him, the final years of his life.

When Father Bede, the Provincial Archivist of the English Dominicans,* asked me to prepare some of Father Geoffrey's conferences for publication, I leapt at the chance. This was because I knew that the work would be for me, in the worn phrase, a labour of love. 'Labour' it certainly was, in that the size of the holdall, crammed to the top with closely-spaced typed pages, and left by Geoffrey when he died, was only commensurable with the physical expanse of its owner. Equally certainly, this labour was 'of love' because, in the simplest possible terms, I did love Geoffrey, and I hold that the *sympathy* of love always gives us deeper access to the one loved. For this reason I presumed that, in one sense at least, I was qualified for the task. 'Sympathy' has become a rather fuzzy word, a softly sentimental word, in our common usage. Generally, it tends to connote no more than a vaguely benevolent concern. But in its origins the words means a co-suffering, a suffering together; and in its development in the living stream of speech it came to mean not a shared suffering in some negative and sterile sense, but a suffering together which moulds us and makes us sensitive, educating us in awareness of the spiritual realities within whose ambience we live. In some ways, I think, this word takes us to the heart of Geoffrey's life. His vocation in the Church, I believe, was essentially that of a sympathiser, one who suffered spiritually with and for others and who therefore could grasp with an extraordinary inwardness a religious tradition which was pivoted on the figure of a Suffering Servant who lived and died in solidarity with all mankind.

Geoffrey used to repeat a remark which the Carmelite nuns of Quiddenham in Norfolk once made to him. St John of the Cross, the great mystical theologian of Carmel, is well-known for his use of the metaphor of the Dark Night to express our relationship with God. The image brings out the painfully obscure character of all authentic growth in holiness. It speaks of how God, if we take him seriously, is for us the hidden God who hides himself and appears to abandon us, in order to deepen our adhesion to him. The Carmelites once suggested to Geoffrey that in our time in the Church the dark night of St John of the Cross is no longer a purely personal, purely individual, experience. Instead, they said, it falls on people as a *corporate* experience, a corporate experience of the Church in the midst of secularism, theological disquiet and doubt, and the collapse of the sense of God. The remark struck Geoffrey, he once told me, very deeply indeed. The way he would refer to it suggests to me that he found in it a key to his own experience, his own life-story, and with that, his own place in the Church. If he could accept in his own person the corporate dark night which had fallen, apparently, on so many Catholics for whom the Lord of Catholicism seemed to be hiding his face; if he could live through, with them and for them, the sense of the absence of God and yet go on trusting, then he could help to redeem them. If he could go on *trusting*: trusting not simply in God as the absolute Good, but in the grace-given capacity of the quite particular Catholic tradition to lead us to God, trusting in the Christ of the Liturgy, the Christ of the saints, the Christ, even, of Thomism, then somehow the task would not just be redemptive of his own life but redemptively influential for other people too. 'No man is an island', wrote John Donne: 'Every spirit is a presence', writes Karl Rahner. And the prophetic human mind of our Lord Jesus Christ could find no better image for the life of discipleship than the vine whose sap courses freely from one branch to another.

Geoffrey's life as a friar and a priest was in many ways an unhappy one. In political terms, his career in the English Dominican Province was largely a failure. In the most crucial office he held, that of novice-master, he found it impossible to sustain the exacting and delicate, and frequently contradictory, demands put upon him. Nor, connected with this, did he succeed in revivifying as he had hoped a sense of the *monastic* values in the Dominican tradition. It seems to me that his brethren should not try to gloss over the elements of waste and failure and sadness in his life; and no amount of posthumous literary glory should be allowed to do so. In terms of the goals he set himself, Geoffrey died disappointed. In Christianity, however, we happen to believe that the image of a failed reformer on a gibbet is the revelation of the character of the God who measured the heavens with a span, and whom Mother Julian of Norwich once saw holding in his hand a tiny nut which, he told her, was 'all that is'. It does not matter that Geoffrey's life was a failure; what matters is what kind of failure it was. Was it or was it not a failure that was redemptive, sanctifying, creative of new life for many people in the Church and on the edges of the Church? It is in this perspective that I myself would wish to see any currency his literary output may come to have.

In Geoffrey's sense of the way of the cross there must have been, I suppose, an element of self-pity, perhaps even of self-indulgence and self-dramatisation. He was a child of Adam. But I find a confirmation of my reading of his life in a homily which he wrote for the feast of All Souls of the Order of Preachers. He wrote there, in a sense, his own obituary:

We have a day dedicated to all souls of the Dominican family, to thinking about the incompleteness of it all, about how it is all so very much short of what it should be and could be. But we stand before God to do so, asking his mercy for one another and each other's mercy and his for ourselves. We stand before God, celebrating the memorial of the sacrifice of Christ, preaching Christ crucified by taking bread and wine and giving thanks over them and breaking the Bread and sharing the Gifts with one another. By making Eucharist faithfully, we preach, we placard, the death of the Lord until he comes; and in doing so we wait for the coming of our Saviour in hope and in joyful hope at that. The incompleteness of it all, our uselessness, the provisional nature of what we are about and where we have got to, all that we acknowledge with regret, but we acknowledge it under the sign of the resurrection of Christ, and because he has risen we believe that we shall rise as well, rise now and at the end.

The dark night of St John of the Cross is a polyvalent metaphor. One of the values the word 'night' carries is that of a secret in the sense of a surprise: this night is 'lovelier than the dawn'. This secret was, for Geoffrey, the person of the Saviour. That year on St Dominic's Day at Holy Cross, Leicester, he said:

> You are not with Jesus only to be useful to him in preaching. There is the sheer delight of being with him. . . . This is what will remain when all the hard slog and study has gone, when the work of preaching will have been completed: just the shared delight in God. That happiness is the goal of it all.

Aidan Nichols OP

*Geoffrey Preston's papers are now housed in the Archives of the English Dominican Province, at St Dominic's Priory, New Bridge Street, Newcastle upon Tyne, NE1 2TH, England.

Advent: the first Sunday[1]

To the liturgical celebration of the coming of God to the world there belongs intrinsically *Advent*, the time of prophecy. For months we have a succession of ordinary Sundays. But then it all changes. Expressed in the external change of colour from green to purple we have a different sort of Sunday, a Sunday with a different feel to it, a different mood and a different significance. We are not left alone in a succession of Sundays after Sundays: we are forced to change. If we are at all sensitive to these matters we are shown time thickening up, changing its depth and density. That is how the Catholic Church constantly behaves. We are not left undisturbed long. We are always being asked to shift ourselves, always being prodded, pushed or pulled. It happens even week by week as the succession of weekdays is interrupted by Sundays, days when we are told that we have different obligations from those that weigh upon us on the other six days, and principally that obligation to be leisurely for twenty-four hours which is more binding and significant for our soul's health than the secondary requirement to celebrate the Mass on Sundays. And just as there are these prods and pulls and pushes by the Church in our individual and shared lives, so there is built into life itself this alternation, shift and movement. We can never simply go on going on. Our lives are marked by occasions when time twists and turns, by moments of higher awareness, spots of time when we have to reconsider the very meaning of our life itself. People we love die. New people come into our lives and change them. Friends are lost. New friends are made. There are high moments, of happiness or sorrow. Our lives are full of moments that will change us. Still, when that happens we can choose to resist the change. We can tell ourselves that life is really smooth and continuous, carrying on uninterruptedly from day to day, week to week, year to year. We may see change as a threat to our well-being because we want 'life' to leave us alone rather than to shift and sift

1

us. If we did not think it irreverent to say what we think, we would like God to get off our backs and leave us alone. We would like to plan our lives in a decorous order. We may want that for the best of reasons, perhaps precisely to be able to serve God better and have more time for him. But then things happen; the pace and arrangement of our lives is altered without our willing it. The time of our lives thickens up. Purple times suddenly interrupt the succession of green days. God sends a prophet, an Isaiah.

Isaiah suggests that the worst thing God could do to us is to leave us alone, to let us be, to allow our lives to run smoothly on through the days and weeks and years. The worst God could do is to stop bothering us. For Isaiah, and in this he is the mouthpiece of his people, God has disappeared from human life. The prayer to him can only be a heartfelt plea that he will return.

> O Lord, why dost thou make us err from thy ways and harden our heart, so that we fear thee not?
> Return for the sake of thy servants, the tribes of thy heritage.[2]

Come back again! Come and start turning our lives upside down again! Anything is better than this absence. It is extraordinary how Isaiah is found alleging that God 'hardens' his people's hearts, and 'makes them err from his ways'. In fact, God hardens hearts simply by not interfering with human lives. He makes his people go astray merely by letting them wander wherever they drift. Anything of value they could do, any return to God and the ways of God they could encompass, any repentance, any melting of their hearts, anything in the way of becoming gentler, more human and humane, that only God can do. Our lives are entirely in God's hand. Our service of God is God's own work in our lives. Our love of God is God loving himself in us and through us. Our turning to God is God turning to us. We cannot turn, we cannot repent except by God's activity. And God may leave us, letting us alone and getting off our backs. Then, left to our own momentum, we are ruined. The law of inertia carries us away, into boredom with God. Our sins like the wind, take us away, if God leaves us alone.

What are we to pray for, then? For God to be an Advent God, an interfering God, a God who will not let us be; for God not to let our lives run smoothly and uneventfully, not to let our old year run out quietly but instead to *come*, to tear the heavens apart if need be; for God to shake us up, to turn us round and round, to be the potter who moulds our lives – anything rather than that he should hold his peace and afflict us so harshly, anything rather than oppress us beyond measure with his silence. The Advent Sequence known as the *Rorate Caeli*, which takes it refrain from Isaiah's appeal, makes all of this plain:

> We have gone astray;
> in the multitude of our sins we have been made unclean.
> Fallen, fallen, stricken as the leaves of autumn.
> The storm wind carries us away,
> the tempest of our evil deeds.
> You have turned away from us the face of your mercy,
> and our iniquity has crushed us like a potter's vessel.

> O Lord our God, look upon your people in their affliction:
> be mindful of your promises.
> Send us the Lamb who will set up his dominion
> from the Rock of the Wilderness to Zion, enthroned on her mountain.
> There is no other whose power can break our chains and set us free.[3]

Next, we pray for ourselves, that we may be able to see what is happening. We pray that we may let God shake us, that we will not hold on to the past, to the lives we have made for ourselves. This includes even the lives of prayer and godly service we have made for ourselves. If God leaves us to ourselves then we are blown away, even if the wind that blows us away is our own goodness and not our sins. 'All our righteous deeds are like a polluted garment',[4] cries Isaiah. Paul too insists on the worthlessness, even the positive harm, of a certain sort of goodness. What matters is not goodness but God. Doing what God requires yet without God will carry us to destruction. That is the nub of what it means to be a pharisee in the gospel sense of that word. The pharisee does what the law of God requires and more, but he does it under his own steam and for his own sake. And God can leave us to ourselves in our goodness with quite as disastrous effect as in leaving us to ourselves in our sin. The servants, each with their own task, get on with their work; but the work matters only in relation to the master. The servants have each their own task through the gifts of the Spirit that have been given to them. Whether these be unusual and striking gifts, or

3

the basic and primary gifts that build up the people of God, there is a demand upon us that we use the talents entrusted to us. But using them, in no matter how good a way, must relate us to God, and not to the gifts in their own right, independently of the Giver.

For the devout, observing, practising Catholic, and for the good person in general, the great danger is that we shall be content with goodness and not perpetually seeking God. That is why so much of the gospel is intended to shake and disturb good people. It is as much the function of the prophet to convert the good as to convict the evil. That is why we must be ready to let ourselves be shaken in the way symbolized by this irruption of Advent into a year which so easily could have been left to fade away gently. That is why we need the voice of Isaiah. The history of the Church shows this clearly: God returning to people who were 'good', so as to force them out of their conventional goodness into a new search for him. God does people the great service of interfering with their lives, of getting on their backs, of shattering the pattern of their lives, of not leaving them alone.

The message of Advent is found in that gospel word which summarises for us Isaiah's challenge: 'Stay awake!'[5] Wake up and stay watchful. Be awake to when God is getting on your back. Stay sensitive to the pulls and pushes and prods, to all God's attempts to dislodge you and make you undertake a pilgrimage of the Absolute. Wake up and stay awake. That distinctive Advent word which can mean 'to pass a sleepless night', 'to watch' or 'to drive sleep away'. We are not to become torpid because life is uneventful. We are not to sleep the sleep of boredom. God is faithful, but the real proof of the faithfulness of God is not that your life keeps on keeping on. On the contrary: you see God being faithful when you find him perpetually interfering in your life and visiting you with his Isaiah.

4

Advent: the second Sunday[6]

When we celebrate the Liturgy we find ourselves referring to the gospel of our Lord Jesus Christ 'according to' Matthew, or Mark or Luke or John. No matter whom it is according to, the gospel is always the good news of Jesus, good news about Jesus and that good news which Jesus is. In any gospel Jesus is first and last. And yet in any gospel we may find ourselves approaching Jesus in the space opened up by the multiple figures who encounter him there. Figures like the Paralysed Man or the Blind Beggar are genuine historical characters, yet their importance for the Liturgy lies in the fact that they are people whose place before Jesus we ourselves can occupy. No doubt they share now in the blessings of the Kingdom; but we do not have to concern ourselves with them as particular people. Rather, they are opportunities for faith. On the other hand, as the time of the Liturgy unfolds we meet New Testament people who belong to the very structure of the gospel as the irreplaceable persons they are. They have in themselves a permanent place in the Church, in the fellowship of the gospel. People like Abraham, Elijah, Mary, Peter and the Twelve have an inalienable position in the Church, and the Liturgy offers us, accordingly, a message about them, even though this message is a part of the message about Jesus and is altogether for the sake of Jesus. One such person is John the Baptist whom the Liturgy highlights in the Advent season. In the first place we concern ourselves with John because of the wholly unique role he played in the working out of God's plan. In the second place, and there only, we see him as a typical example of the holiness involved in preparing the way of the Lord.

It may seem odd to many that the Church should make such a fuss of John the Baptist. It would not have seemed odd to our medieval forebears in the faith, anymore than it would to Orthodox Christians today. It was John who sat at the side of Jesus in the paintings of the Last Judgement, in an intimacy shared only with

5

Mary, the two of them pleading for the world that Christ has redeemed and that he now judges. John, they would have said, is to be honoured because his life formed the immediate preparation for the coming of Christ. He was the high point of all the centuries of making ready for the Messiah. In John the voice of prophecy, so long silent, spoke again with all its old accents of demand for repentance, for turning back to God, but also with a novel note of urgency. The need is so much greater now: the Lord is at hand. John is the archetypal preacher of repentance. He binds, so that Jesus might loose. He consigns all things to sin, that is, he says that the whole world lies under the power of sin, so that those who believe may receive the promised gift, given through faith in Christ. That is what his baptism was about. It was the custom for Gentiles who wished to become Jews to be baptized, probably to give them a taste of that Exodus experience of passing through the sea which had made Israel a people. John's message was that Israel too needed to be baptized. He was, we might say, the first Catholic, for he was the first to affirm, with all possible vigour, that Israel and the nations were as one before God. God can raise up children to Abraham from these very stones on the river's bank. John focusses the call to repentance, the need to know oneself and one's failure, to acknowledge one's sinfulness and one's particular sin. He stands in Scripture and in the Church as the one who refracts that element with particular brilliance, the greatest amongst those born of women. Without him the gospel is incomplete, even though the least in the Kingdom of Heaven is greater than he. Without his conviction of sin, Christ's full and free forgiveness, the grace abounding, is so much cheaper.

We may grasp better John's relation to Jesus if we study our own experience of confession. John's ministry images that moment which is called the binding, the acknowledgement that I have done such and such, and that such and such is indeed sinful and that I have done it through my fault, through my own most grievous fault. Without that moment of binding the moment of absolution, the unloosing, can make no sense. The point of confession is forgiveness: but forgiveness is appropriate only when there is something to forgive. So often what we say in confession cries out for understanding; we can be excused from what we have done, for the mitigating circumstances are so many. But the sacrament comes into its own as the grace abounding of the cross of Christ only when it has its moment of John the Baptist, that moment which makes ready a people that is prepared because it knows its need. There is a world of difference between excusing a wrong deed and forgiving it. Often enough it is right to excuse; but only if we see that there are times when there can be no question of anything except forgiveness do we appreciate how God in Christ has reconciled us to himself. And to see that, we must look at John the Baptist preaching and convicting the world of sin in order that he may point thereby at the Lamb of God who takes the sin of the world away.

What John had to do, and managed to do, for the sake of us all was to point to Jesus. That too is a moment in the coming of Jesus into the world. John belongs to the mystery of the coming of God amongst us, that past event and that present reality. Sunday by Sunday in the Liturgy we sing: 'Blessed is he who is coming in the name of the Lord.'[7] 'The One who is coming'[8] is one of the titles of the Word of God: it is his proper name. If we want to know how he comes, how to recognize the signs and forms of his appearing in our late twentieth-century world, then we look to the pattern of his appearing shown when he came those two thousand years ago. God's Word and Son exists for ever. In the beginning he did not come or become: he simply was. Yet the marvel of it is that he who was and who is, eternally the same, actually came amongst us. The Word happened in time. And as he occurred in flesh so a man, John, turned up, sent from God. And what happened there and then shows us what happens whenever the Word of God happens on our world. John cannot be disassociated from Jesus. John points to Jesus with the words, 'Behold the Lamb of God.'[9] He is a finger and a voice, as in the great Grünewald painting of the Crucifixion where he stands by the Crucified and points to him with that enormously elongated finger. All that it meant for him to be who and what he was is in that finger. That continues to be his role in the Church, pointing away from himself and towards Jesus. 'Behold the Lamb of God': his words remain the model words used in the Western Mass for the minister to point away from himself and towards the sacrament of the crucified Jesus. Had John not first pointed him out, had he not indicated him at that critical moment, then we could not have heard the good news. Without John, Advent cannot hasten towards Christmas; without him we could not hallow all our times.

The Chinese have a saying: 'The sun does not need a bell to announce its shining.' Yet the Life which is the Light of men needs a witness, the finger and the voice of the Baptist, a voice still

7

resonating as Advent reaches the third of its Sundays. The Word of God does not force himself on our attention, still less does he compel our assent to him. He is seen not by his own shining but in the life that men and women live together. We do not create the Light: we are not the Light. But unless we point to the Light, the Light is not seen nor may anything be seen in its light. This relation of John to Jesus, ambiguous, paradoxical, riddling, equivocal and contentious, represents the relation of each and of all of us to Jesus, the relation of Christ to his Church. 'John was not the Light',[10] says the prologue to the Fourth Gospel. But elsewhere in that gospel Jesus calls John that 'lamp that burns and that shines'.[11] John was not Elijah, according to his own testimony. But Jesus says, 'If you are willing to receive him, this is Elijah who is to come.'[12] John is not the prophet, he says. But Jesus says of him that he is 'a prophet, yes and much more than a prophet'.[13] Among those born of women, in the judgement of Jesus, 'there has not arisen a greater than John the Baptist'.[14] Jesus is fulsome in his praise of John. But the gospels surround him with negatives. John is both an enigma, and a person with whom we must come to terms if we are going to hold and live the full gospel of Christ. So we must come to terms with him this Advent, the equivocal John who both *is* and *is not*.

That means coming to terms with our own calling as a Church, for this is what John represents. We too both *are* and *are not*. We have to be such a community as points to the Light: that is our function in the world. Not that we save ourselves, or produce Christ in the world; but we have to point to and point up the Light that is already shining, the Light of the world which happened as a man, in Jesus of Nazareth, and which is still occurring. The possibility is always there that we may succeed in pointing only to ourselves as, apparently for some men in the Palestine of the time of Jesus, John only pointed to himself. They mistook him for the Light itself and did not pass over to following Jesus when the time for that came. It is surely a sign of John's greatness and of his faithfulness to his mission that the New Testament had to play down his significance. And we too, the Church, are challenged to be John to Jesus Christ in such a way that others might even mistake us for the Light itself. At the moment the likelihood is rather that people wonder how Jesus ever came to be mixed up with men and women like us. If we are no kind of sign it is doubtful whether the world will meet Jesus himself, for he is encountered and believed in through the witness of people like ourselves. Without a way of life

8

that is arresting, drawing attention to itself despite its wish to draw attention to Jesus only, Jesus will go on standing in the midst of our world as one whom people do not know.

Advent: the third Sunday[15]

Today the Lectionary places before us the prophet Zephaniah's oracle of jubilation over the virgin Israel as she comes to meet her God on the day of salvation:

> Sing aloud, O daughter of Zion;
>   shout, O Israel!
> Rejoice and exult with all your heart,
>   O daughter of Jerusalem.
>   The Lord has taken away the judgements against you,
>   he has cast out your enemies.
> The King of Israel, the Lord, is in your midst;
>   you shall fear evil no more.[16]

As Advent draws on, the praying Church comes to see that expectancy of the virgin daughter of Zion, the Old Testament people of God, focussed more and more sharply in a single Jewish virgin, Mary of Nazareth, in whom all the believing and the hoping of the Israel of old is summed up.

Towards the end of his life Karl Barth was asked whether he had changed his mind on any important matter during the course of his life. He said that there was one point in particular on which he had shifted his opinions. Once he believed that Jesus of Nazareth came to preach the Kingdom of God. Now he knew that Jesus *was* that Kingdom. Origen had seen it all so many centuries before: *autobasileia*, himself the Kingdom. In his person Jesus was the reign of God in the world, God being gracious, God coming with healing and forgiveness. In meeting Jesus we encounter the Kingdom of God, as people found God-for-them when they met him in the streets and the countryside of Palestine. When we meet Jesus in word, sacrament or neighbour, then we find the Kingdom of God. The man of flesh and blood like ours, in whom our human nature

10

was taken into the Godhead, is personally the Kingdom. And so anything that served the en-fleshing of Jesus was a service of the Kingdom of God. That is why those quite unsavoury goings-on between Judah and Tamar are recounted without demur in the book of Genesis: for had they not been, the Messiah could never have come. Now the person who most immediately and directly served the taking of our flesh by the Word of God was Mary. She stands at the midmost point of the enmanment of God. By serving the taking of our nature by the Son of God, she put herself at the service of the Kingdom of God which we have entered and in another sense shall come to enter.

Mary has a special relationship to the Kingdom because she has a special relationship to the King. She is his mother and, by definition, uniquely so. And yet the gospels insist that any Christian is his mother (or sister, or brother), that what matters most is not the unique way of being his mother but the common way, not the altogether unparallelled charism but the universal gift. And so in Mary too what matters most is what she has in common with us, not what makes her different. And what she has in common with us is her faith. 'Blessed is she who believed!'[17] In looking at her we see faith as it should be with us. In looking at other believers we see faith as it must have been with her. What we praise in her is just such faith. To praise her adequately, we do not necessarily need to find exceptional characteristics or privileges but rather to appreciate properly the immense privilege there is in being a Christian, the immense privilege there would be even if the whole world were Christian. And the heart of Mary's common privilege, the moment that made her the perfect virgin daughter of Zion and so the first properly Christian believer, is her response of faith to the Angel. 'Be it done to me according to your word.'[18] Extraordinary the gift of words. Extraordinary that they can come to us bringing the past with them, so that we can never speak without our thoughts being determined to some degree by the talk of the past. But how much more amazing that words can throw a line over the future. The truly astonishing power of words lies not in repeating what we have heard, but in a person being able to project days and years to come, even a lifetime to come. A person can say, 'I will', taking account of what is not yet and covering it in his intent. This is what Mary does at the annunciation. She says a 'Yes' to God's word which will determine the rest of her life in ways she could not have foreseen. She could not know what the future held, even though she

11

knew who held the future. And we, like her, can cast nets in rivers north of the future. We forget how strange it is that there are any future tenses of verbs, how queer it is that we can make coherent utterances that bind tomorrow. It is so mysterious, this faculty of promising which Nietzsche called 'the memory of the will'. As Mary committed her future to the Word of God which Gabriel represents, so any one of us can commit himself to a lifetime with other particular persons who in turn commit themselves to him.

This kind of self-commital does not mean, of course, that all our problems are solved and all eventualities covered. Quite the opposite. If you promise to share a person's life and give him the right to share yours, then by that fact alone you have opened yourself to continual change. Mary put herself at the service of the Kingdom which was Jesus himself, the flesh-and-blood man from Nazareth. We put ourselves at the service of his kingdom, of Jesus as he comes to us in others, in our communities and in the people we teach, or preach to, or care for. Such service as this depends on no force. It turns rather on a free agreement, on contracts, treaties, covenants, which leave life unpredictable in order that God's will may be done. And yet our promises and commitments to the Lord's will in saying that Marian 'Yes' create in our lives islands of certainty. Only we must not use these to imperialize the whole ground of the future, winning a path secure in all directions. That would defeat the whole enterprise. The security of commitment is not to make us less of a pilgrim, as Abraham, our father in faith, was a pilgrim, but more so. (It seems sometimes that Abraham left Ur for no other reason than to try out the power of mutual promise in the wilderness of the world. His whole story shows a passionate drive towards making covenants, until eventually God himself made a covenant with him.)

By saying 'Yes' to God, 'Be it done to me according to your word!', we relinquish a certain control of our lives. The other person comes to us, and life itself henceforth comes to us, in such a way that we cannot twist away from it. Or at least we cannot if we hold to the commitment made and live within the *Yes* that Mary said on behalf of all human nature. It brings suffering in the ancient sense of that word. Life comes to us and we, on the receiving end, take it with what Wordsworth called 'wise passiveness'. It may involve suffering in the modern sense. It *will* involve such suffering. To take life you have to be able to 'take it', as we say. And yet the pain is incidental to the acceptance, to the both-handed taking. We can have little idea where that will lead. In the nature of things we could not have, because we are involved in this with other people, who are themselves centres of freedom. Through these other people, loved, no doubt, but loved with both eyes open, God shapes our lives. We can only commit ourselves to God as we commit ourselves to other people, just as Mary committed herself both to Joseph and to the child she was conceiving. What comes of our lives is God's concern. All such Christian living is not a career but a vocation. A career you carve out for yourself and busy yourself about, but a vocation you receive. It comes to you like life and as life. A successful career is not a Christian ideal although it may be compatible with being a Christian. But if we do not know where our vocational 'Yes' will lead we do at any rate know a good deal of where it has come from, our own past and the past of Israel and of the Church. It is to that past that we allude when we commemorate the presentation of Mary in the Temple. The past of Israel was summed up in Mary saying her 'Yes' within the tradition of Israel, just as the past is summed up in our own 'Yes' which is always given in the context of some particular style of Christian living, handed on across the generations. The moment of saying 'Yes' is a gathered moment, a recollected moment. You gather yourself, and collect your past, all that is good and holy and right and true about your infancy and childhood and the years a-growing. You gather them as the wheat scattered on the hillsides is gathered for bread. You take them in your hand, the young-time and the sap-years. But you do so only in order to give them up and to hand them over. Vintage years you can bottle, but only so that they can be uncorked. What was laid up must be poured out for others' delight. You give the gathered into someone else's hands, as really as if you hated it all. The bread will be taken and held and broken in the pattern of the Mass. Only then, according to that pattern, will it come back to you, the gathered years transformed, eternally valid. Cling to them, and you will lose them. Give them up, and they are yours to enjoy in a new way. And all of this is what we should be learning when we contemplate Mary of Nazareth.

Advent: the fourth Sunday

This week the Church begins to sing that great series of Advent acclamations to Christ known as the 'O Antiphons'. She crams into these texts, the seven Os, all that Advent means and all that Advent is. And Advent is not so much a season of the Church's year, an annual recurrence, as one aspect of the whole of our Christian living, an element which has to soak through and through the whole of our lives before God in the world. We are Advent, just as we are Easter. Just as we are Easter, dead and buried with Christ and risen with him, so we are Advent, we are expectation, the longing which Christ still is. 'Christ longed to hallow the world with his merciful coming',[19] the Christmas Martyrology tells us. At the last supper he said that he had longed and longed to eat that meal with his disciples before he suffered, hungering and thirsting for that moment, full of expectation. We learn from the apostle that even now, when he is seated at the right hand of God, he waits expectantly until his enemies be made a stool for his feet. The Christ who is seated at the right hand of God, the Christ who is Lord and King, still prays to the Father for the coming of his kingdom and for the resurrection of his body, for the great and general resurrection, the transfiguration of the world. For us to be Advent is for us to share in that prayer of Christ for the coming of God's kingdom. It is indifferent whether we pray 'Your kingdom come' or whether we pray 'Come, Lord Jesus', for the kingdom is a king, and the king is his kingdom. In the *Our Father* we pray for our interim needs, our daily bread, the nourishment we need to keep us going from day to day, only when we have prayed for what we really want, the coming of God's kingdom. Day by day, and all the time, we have to pray for that. Day by day, all the time, we have to be Advent, expectation, because the Lord is Advent and expectation and we have to put on Christ, the whole Christ. The contemplative man, as the medieval Church put it, is *suspensus expectatione*, taut like a bow-

14

string with expectation. The person who tries to let Christ take over his whole life is going to become like the Christ who is also keyed up with longing. It is indifferent whether that longing be expressed in prayer to the Father in the style of the Lord's Prayer, or whether we turn our gaze to Jesus himself and pray him to come and save us. As in the Eucharist, though the dominant mode in prayer is prayer to the Father, through, with and in Christ, yet we do from time to time turn and face Christ directly, calling out to him to be gracious to us, to hear our prayer and to grant us peace. And so in Advent too we pray the Father to send his Christ, his Messiah; and equally we turn directly to the Messiah and pray him to come.

In the Great Antiphons of Advent we turn to Christ with the longing expressed in the O itself. This longing is the groaning of the Holy Spirit in us when we do not know how to pray, when we have no other words than this primordial word so close to the roots of our western experience. For our O is strictly comparable to the Hindu OM, the mystic syllable of that other part of our Indo-European tradition, the OM beyond which there vibrates that absolutely primordial and eternal unheard sound which is itself the first Cause of the universe. The Advent Os of the Christian West go back at least to the eighth century, to those ages that we somewhat inaccurately, yet appropriately in this context, call 'dark'. From the dark ages men have called out to Messiah to come, not at all sure just where they were, not at all clear about their surroundings. We too as we sing these antiphons stand in the dark ages, *vergente mundi vespere* as the Office Hymn puts it, as earth draws near its evening hour'.[20] We pray for him to come, although we know that he has already come through Mary so that he is not an unknown quantity, but the Jesus who has been one of us for two thousand years. So we pray for him to come at either end of the Song of Mary, the *Magnificat*. We put all we have into that praying. In the monastic tradition it is surrounded by all the wealth of ceremonial of which the brethren are capable, a richness which only makes more poignant the emptiness that the words express. In monasteries the abbot himself in full pontifical vestments comes and stands before the great pulpit in the midst of the choir and intones *O Sapientia*. Night after night the senior members of the community in full vestments come out to take up the cry to the Messiah. The bells of the monastery sound throughout the singing of the *Magnificat*, sung as it is to the most solemn chant in the book. All that the community has to show for itself, all by which it might

15

cut something of a figure in the world, is wheeled on; and it sings, 'O come!' Just as there is a wordless jubilation of rejoicing at Easter, as the last syllable of the *Alleluia* is held and played with, so there is a wordless *jubilus* of expectation now. Perhaps all that the antiphons of these last few days before Christmas were in the beginning was just such a long, drawn-out, wordless cry of longing and expectation.

The O indeed is an emptiness. We must be careful not to fill that emptiness with our own chatter and fussiness, with our compromises and comforts. The O is an exercise in making space for God alone, *soli Deo vacare*. But it is a space that he can and does fill with his presence. We make space for God in our hearts, trying to want only him, in the expectation that when he comes to fill whatever space we have made for him he will elbow his way round a bit and enlarge our little capacity for love. After all, our O is only the echo in time of the eternal O of God. It is because God longs for us that we thirst for him. St Gregory Nazianzen teaches that the cause of our thirst for God is God's own thirsting for our thirst. Our thirst and longing for him is the vocalization of the longing of the universe for God. Our prayer for him to come is the voice of the creation to which we belong and for which we are responsible and which is frustrated, pointless, insignificant, meaningless until we mean what we are meant to mean and find ourselves in finding the God to whom we call, 'Come!' Our repeated 'Come!' answers to the repeated 'Come!' of the Lord in Scripture: Come from Libanus, come and be crowned; Abraham, come to the land that I will show you; Lazarus, come forth; Arise my love, my fair one, and come away; come follow me, Peter, Andrew, James, John; come to me all who are weary and heavy-laden. . . . The history of all God's dealings with us can be read as a history of those repeated calls backwards and forwards between man and God. We can fairly expect, then, that God will start to fill and to expand the emptiness of the O as soon as we create it. We do not only have the future to look forward to. We have the present to rejoice in, the present which is already big with the future of the world. That present future of all things is the Christ to whom we cry out in these antiphons, just as Mary was already big with him when she sang that *Magnificat* which they accompany. Tomorrow is already. We can begin to live in the tomorrow of our longings even as we still give voice to them. The promise of tomorrow is there in our very calling out to Messiah. There is a literary conceit in the antiphons which makes this point well. Read them in reverse order, from 23 December to 17 December, and the initial letters of the names by which we call on Christ spell out the promise that Christ is already making to us: ERO CRAS. I will be tomorrow. There is that about God which is future to us: he will be tomorrow. We cannot get him taped and sealed down. We have to be ready for what he will be, for the unexpected things he may turn out to be. We have to beware of domesticating him. But he *will* be tomorrow. The promise is there as well. Don't try to pin him down too much on details, but don't get so agnostic that you lose all hope of anything other than what you have already. There is a delicate balance in all this between our expectations and the God who comes to burst all our expectations open.

O Sapientia: 17 December

And so on this first day of the O Antiphons we sing:

> O Wisdom, you come forth from the mouth of the Most High.
> You fill the universe and hold all things together in a strong yet
> gentle manner. O come to teach us the way of prudence.

We sing to the Wisdom that spoke for itself in the Old Testament,
opening her mouth in the assembly of the Most High. Specifically,
we call on Wisdom in the words of Jesus ben-Sirach, words originally written a couple of hundred years before the birth of Jesus of
Nazareth and later translated by ben-Sirach's grandson into the
book as we have it now. Such wisdom books as his represent a
category of writing that flourished in the Ancient East. Although
the work of the Far East was unknown to the biblical writers, the
wisdom books of the Near East had a considerable and direct
influence on them, so much so that we have largish chunks of
straight quotations from the pagan authors in a book like Proverbs.
So in praying this antiphon for Wisdom we pray in some pretty
mixed company. Outside Israel indeed, and often enough within
Israel too, the wisdom such writers were concerned with was simply
the kind of wisdom required for making your way in the world.
They tried to offer a recipe for successful living. In a sort of Dale
Carnegie way they offered advice on how to get on, or at least to
get by, in the world. All this sounds and is very humanistic, but it
is included in Scripture (as the Song of Songs is included) as a valid
area of human experience. It is as the men and women we are that
we come before God, praying Messiah to come. We are people with
whole areas of experience that have no obvious and immediate
religious significance. Such areas are, we say, secular, belonging to
this world. Yet it was this world that God so loved that he sent his
Son, his Wisdom, into it. Jesus ben-Sirach, however, was not sat-

isfied with this business of merely telling people how to cope with the exigencies of daily life. He looked for a way to unify his whole experience as a Jew. He wanted to unify the past and the future of his nation before God, and to unify the inter-relationship of God and the individual with the day-to-day affairs of living in the world, getting on or at least getting by. This way can be found in the idea of Wisdom, for Wisdom, he says, can be found in God himself; it is written into the very structure of the world; and it is offered to everybody, but especially to those who love God. This discovery of his set the pattern for all subsequent reflection in the Jewish–Christian tradition on the unity of God's work in creation, providence and redemption. Probably there is no final answer as to just how the whole of our experience is ultimately a unity. That quest is a task which each new generation has to work out for itself, as our experience of the world alters in those 'subtle ways of wisdom' that ben-Sirach talks about. The world for us is interpreted in ever new ways, in new scientific theories, in the advances in physical, psychological and sociological disciplines, in new art-forms, in new techniques of communication and the rest. A previous generation would not have been able to see the world as we see it, to have our sense of time-scale and space-scale. For a previous generation the world as a human construct (and the world is always to quite a degree a human construct) was really different. And so we are constantly being asked to find out *how* (and not only *that*) the God who creates and sustains and redeems is *one* God, how he speaks only the one Word through whom all things were made, in whom all things hold together and who was translated into flesh and blood in a particular historical individual, in Jesus of Nazareth.

We pray to wisdom to come, and to teach. *Veni ad docendum*: come in order to teach and because you want to teach. If we are going to be taught by Wisdom herself we have to be ready to be taught by people and situations, for Wisdom reaches mightily from one end of the earth to the other and gently orders all things. The Wisdom which is incarnate in Jesus of Nazareth is not a different wisdom from that which underlies the laws of nature and the laws of human nature and the events of history. If we tried to learn only from some supernatural wisdom which was not available in the world of history and nature and other people, then it would not be the Wisdom to which we sing in Advent that would be teaching us. The Wisdom to which we sing reaches mightily from one end of the earth to the other, and the more we enlarge our sympathies to reach out like

19

Wisdom the more likely our chance of hearing the echoes of its voice and learning from it. Human culture *can* be an obstacle to those dispositions which enable us to hear Wisdom's voice, but more frequently the hurdles lie with our inadequate sympathies, our over-narrow range of interests. It is false to our Christian tradition, it is unwise, to try to flee from the world which God loved so much that he sent his Son, his Wisdom, to it. It is wise to flee from the world that is at enmity with God, but that world is what we have made of the world. It is the world we have made against God, made out of our enmity with God, and not the world as such. The desire for God cannot bypass a reverence and respect and indeed a love for what God in his Wisdom has created, and created good, and created very good.

And what we want to learn from Wisdom, surprisingly enough at first sight, is the way of *prudence*. When we call on the Wisdom that is co-eternal with the Father, proceeding from the mouth of the Most High, it seems banal to ask first of all for instruction in, of all things, prudence. Yet there is nothing we can more properly ask of Wisdom than how to be prudent. Only if we have prudence, that is, discretion, discernment, a sense of the realities of things and persons and situations, can we give a welcome to Wisdom. Catherine of Siena, meditating on the story of the annunciation when Eternal Wisdom did come first, sees Mary as exercising the virtue of prudence in her conversation with the Angel. Prudence made her ask the right questions and prudence enabled her to give the appropriate reply. In classical Christian ethics it is said that you cannot be good at all unless you are prudent at the same time. No matter how good or holy what you do or say might be in the abstract, it is only really good if it is prudent, done at the right time, in the right situation, with the right person. It is not enough for us just to be sincere in what we do. If what we do is a silly thing to do in that situation, if we over-react or under-react or react inappropriately, then we are not being good. And so we pray first of all to be taught the way of prudence, to be taught how to live a life that is in all things pleasing to God, how to become a saint. Prudence is not all there is to be said about Christian living, but without prudence there can be nothing else. Teresa of Avila used to say that if a girl were sensible she could make her good, but that only God could make a girl sensible. Ask God to teach you the way of prudence, how to behave in the appropriate way along the ordinary paths of this earth. It was those common paths which Jesus of Nazareth trod and, in treading, became the Way itself, the way which led up to Jerusalem and which once led and still leads to the Father. How eloquent are those paths, that way of prudence, that simple and uncomplicated form of life which does not bother so much with special charisms and particular ways that it forgets ordinary human virtues; does not live in the lofty ways of charity in such a way that it ignores honest straight-forward justice; does not allow monastic virtues to replace Christian ones.

It is eternal Wisdom whom we pray to come and teach us the way of prudence. Ordinary prudence comes from eternal Wisdom. We may fairly expect that by looking towards him we will discover how to be prudent. In its most palpable form this looking is towards him as he was and is embodied in the flesh and blood of Jesus of Nazareth, the risen and glorified Christ of our faith. We learn the way of prudence by studying the book of Christ crucified in which Bonaventure told Thomas Aquinas he had learned all his wisdom. We learn the way of prudence by having the Lord so much before us that he becomes us. We stand eventually not before him but with him, with him before the Father and with him before one another, praying and working alike with him.

O Adonai: 18 December

Today the Church sings at Vespers:

O Adonai, leader of the house of Israel, who appeared to Moses
in the fire of the burning bush and gave him the Law on Sinai:
come to redeem us with an outstretched arm.

Nowadays we sometimes come across the Hebrew proper name for
God in our modern translations: *Yahweh*, as it is often spelt. In fact
we cannot be sure that that was how it was pronounced for it had
ceased to be pronounced openly before the time of Jesus, except
once a year and that by the High Priest in the Holy of Holies on
Yom Kippur, the Day of Atonement. When it was met with in the
Hebrew text of Scripture the reader, rather than articulate this
awesome name of God, read *Adonai*, the Lord. Thus when we call
upon the Lord as *Adonai* we are meant to be conscious of the
altogether awesome nature of God. We should be aware of God as
altogether other, the Mystery that makes men shudder yet fascinates
them. There is that about God which makes it impossible for us to
approach him and which does not let us even name him by his own
name for fear of what might happen to us. This is not just some
antiquated Old Testament idea. Think of how in the New Testament people are afraid at what Jesus does, at the manifestations of
the action of God in the person and activities of Jesus. Luke's
Gospel in particular is full of people being filled with such awe.
There is a fear of the Lord, a respect and sense of otherness which
will never become redundant for it is the beginning of wisdom. It
is a fearsome thing we do, taking on God, wrestling with the living
God, in prayer or in Eucharist. True, he has given us a slight help
and handicapped himself in that he has become one of us by the
incarnation, when he made himself vulnerable and able to be
thrown in the wrestling match. But though he has taken what he

did not have, our vulnerability, he has not lost what he always had, his godhead, his awesomeness. It is a fearful thing to fall into the hands of the living God, to have to wrestle with him. He will wound us and send us off limping, conscious of our own poverty and helplessness. He lets us call him *Adonai* or 'Jesus'. The Ground of Being and the Granite of it lets us call him 'Father' and gives himself a more human scale. But if we do not have a salutary sense of caution and a sense of the otherness of God as we approach him, he will himself instil it in the painful form of letting us taste our own poverty and impotence in prayer. He will leave us to our own devices until we learn how his ways are not our ways nor our thoughts his thoughts.

Yet we do want him to come, *Adonai*, the human face of God, the human and everyday pronunciation of the name which no one can pronounce and live. *Adonai*, the way we say the name which God revealed to Moses at the burning bush.

> 'If I come to the people of Israel and say to them: "The God of your fathers has sent me to you", and they ask me, "What is his name?", what shall I say to them?' God said to Moses, 'I am who I am: say this to the people of Israel, "I Am has sent me to you". '[21]

The God whom we can name without fear of polluting our lips in naming him is none other than the God who revealed his inexpressible name to Moses in the burning bush. When he comes, our reaction must be like that of Moses who put off the shoes from his feet and who hid his face in his mantle. He put off his shoes not only as a sign of poverty but also as a sign of being able to come before God only as the man he was. Being barefoot is a sign and part of the necessary avoidance of pretence and pretentiousness. So Moses put off the shoes from his feet and hid his face, presumably covering it with his mantle as Elijah did in his cave. He hid his face so that he could hear better and not be distracted by seeing, as the Carthusians do during the Canon of the Mass, pulling their great hoods down over their faces. God appeared to Moses in the burning bush by speaking to Moses. There is our God: the true God can be heard but not seen, while the gods of the heathen can be seen, but they cannot speak, they are dumb. For us, even when there are visions they must become words so that they can be the motive for activity. 'Write the vision',[22] Habakkuk is told; John on Patmos is instructed, 'Write down all that you see.'[23] And in the conversation God tells Moses the way to go. Yet not only that: he leads the way, going before him in a pillar of fire and cloud as *dux domus Israel*, the leader of the House of Israel. God goes first and the people follow, as in all discipleship. Our God is the God who tells us what we are to do, calling us to follow him and demanding discipleship from us.

After the Exodus God leads Moses and the people to Sinai, to the mountain where he would give the Law to Moses. Notice that the keeping of the Law was not a precondition for their being rescued from Egypt. That had happened already. It was, rather, the statement of the appropriate response to the rescue. That is the pattern in both Old and New Testaments. God's work of redemption is not a reward for getting through the obstacle course of the Law and arriving more or less intact at the other end. The Law is the response for those who have been brought out of slavery into freedom, for those who want to be so free that they can will one thing with God himself. Keeping the Law is our way of showing our gratitude to God. The Law in showing us the will of God, so far from being some arbitrary statement, shows us God himself. Such and such is our God. To will one will with God is to love God, but 'we love because he has first loved us',[24] not in order to try and force him into loving us. This is true above all in the New Law which is the very grace of the Holy Spirit. It applies not only to those guides for using God's grace aright that we find in the Scriptures but also to whatever rule of life we live by. For instance, those of us who live by monastic Rules should keep them not in order to make ourselves acceptable to God but so as to render love for love, loving because he first loved us. Notice that it is not that we love *him* because he first loved us (as the text is often mis-translated); it is simply that we love because he first loved us. Our love for one another, expressed in following the common life where we both assist one another and leave one another alone, is a response of gratitude for having first been loved by this God who appeared to Moses in the fire of the burning bush and who gave him the Law on Sinai. The sheer gratuitousness of the appearance of God to Moses in the bush has its outcome in the sheer gratuitousness of his *gift* of the Law on Sinai. To Moses, and so to us, on the heights of Sinai as on the heights of the Upper Room of Pentecost, God has graciously granted insight into his very own freedom so that the people could learn to be free with the liberty of God.

To this God, *Adonai*, we sing, 'Come!' May he come now as he came then as fire and as guide along the way. For the Fathers of the Church, God is the God who always appears in the burning bush, in the burning bush which is Israel and in the burning bush which is Mary. First of all he appears in Israel, the people who have burnt in the fires of the persecutions which in every generation men have raised against her. Israel has burnt in the fiery furnaces of Egypt and of Babylon and of the ghettoes set alight by European Christians in the Middle Ages as in the furnace of the gas-ovens of cultured Christian twentieth-century Germany. In the Israel of old and in modern Jewry God appears to those who have eyes to see. He remains true to his first love there, continuing to epiphanize in the bush which continues to burn and to be. Israel is perhaps the one pragmatic proof of the existence of the God in whom we profess our faith. Can we ever recognize the great debt we owe to a people who have let God appear in them as Israel has? At least as we sing the Advent antiphons we can remember how our life is rooted in the life of Israel. We can remember that we are praying with Israel and for Israel as we pray for the coming of Messiah whom she awaits as much as we, even though she does not know that his human name is Jesus.

Finally, we speak of our God as appearing in the burning bush which is Mary. The liturgy describes her thus in her Solemnity on 1 January, in keeping with the way the Eastern Church depicts her in its icons. Mary, her virginity burning with the fire of the Holy Spirit, but not consumed. Mary, afire with God but not burned out with his love. Mary, whose whole significance was and is that the fire should burn in her, leading people to say as Moses said, 'I will turn aside and see this great sight, why the bush is not consumed.'[25] This text was anciently sung as an antiphon on the feast of the Expectation of the Virgin, on 18 December, when the Church celebrated Mary as *suspensus expectatione*, taut with expectation. She is the model and source of all contemplatives, of those whose being is a waiting for the coming of God to fill their emptiness. The angel Gabriel was sent from God to a virgin, to somebody who had nothing to show for herself, in a city about which nothing good was ever said. The only point to Mary lay contained in the angel's message, just as the only point to Nazareth was that the Word should be made flesh there. Mary's utter openness, that lack of any other hope than God, that asking one thing alone of the Lord, was answered by God at the incarnation when he came to ransom it all, to speak up for it and to be its *go'el*, its redeemer and advocate.

25

Mary, the expectant and contemplative one, found her fulfilment there.

Because of that unity of her life around its one desire, the gospel of the Mary who was sister to Martha and Lazarus used to be read, quote appropriately, on Marian feasts. Mary the mother of Jesus was the woman who more than any other paid attention to one thing alone and found her meaning only in one thing, or rather in one person, *Adonai*, the Wisdom of God. It has long been a common thing to use Martha and Mary as types of two life-styles in the Church, Martha standing for the active life, labouring at works of loving service for her brethren, and Mary standing for the contemplative, with leisure to sit and listen to the words of Jesus. We are all vaguely aware nowadays that this will not do as a way of talking about contemplation and activity. Mary of Nazareth overcomes any such dichotomy. She is the model for both the contemplative and the active styles of life as well as for the unity of the two sides of loving service of the brethren and loving attention to the Word of God in the lives of each of us as individuals. That is why she has been called 'the philosophy of Christians'. No one was ever such a Martha in serving as Mary of Nazareth was, ministering to the humanity of the Word not only out of the good things she possessed but out of her very substance, giving her flesh and blood to be his, offering him the hospitality not simply of her home but of her body. She nursed him, cared for him and got him away safely from Herod. After Martha had done all her ministering, there was Mary, standing by him at the cross, present at his burial. And yet she was *the* contemplative. No one else was such a contemplative that she had the Godhead itself in her very body, making flesh of the Word of God who was in the beginning with God and who was God. In her own flesh and blood she could at once contemplate the glory of the divinity and serve him. For her there was no distance between the way of devotion to God and the way of loving service of man. And so we can ask the *Adonai* who showed himself in the burning bush that was Mary to come to us also in a way consistent with that way he once came. We beg him to come and teach us how to be places of his presence, setting us on fire with the Holy Spirit and yet not burning us out. We pray him to come and ransom us with an outstretched arm, as he ransomed Israel out of Egypt's land. And he will do so, for 'he stretched out his arms on the cross; he put an end to death and revealed the resurrection'.[26]

O Radix Jesse: 19 December

In the crucifixion we see *Adonai* himself judging and saving us, inviting us to accept his judgement and to be saved by it as we accept that God's judgement on Christ is his judgement on us as well. That judgement condemns us to death and raises us from death, and we have to stretch out our arms to him as he stretches out his arms to us. We have to recognize ourselves in him and him in ourselves, trying to be where he is in order to share his destiny. But we can be where he is only because he is where we are. Eternal Wisdom proceeds from the mouth of the Most High, but he proceeds also from the bodies of countless generations of men and women in Israel. He is one of us and there is cause for joy in that fact. Hence the song of the Church today at Vespers:

O shoot of Jesse, who stand as an ensign for the peoples, before whom kings shall shut their mouths, whom the gentiles shall seek after, come to deliver us. Delay now no longer.

The genealogy of Jesus is part of the good news of the gospel, solemnly chanted at Christmas and at Epiphany. To sing somebody's family tree in public is hardly an obvious thing to do: most families have a few skeletons in their cupboard, a few *bars sinister* on their coats of arms. Somewhere in a family there is usually a scandal, a few generations back if not a few years. Yet on Christmas night and on the night of the Epiphany the family tree of Jesus is sung by the Church to a marvellous chant that lingers over each syllable of the names of his ancestors, to the accompaniment of full ceremonial, lights, incense and vestments, 'The Book of the Genesis of Jesus Christ, the Son of David, the Son of Abraham'.[27] Either this, Matthew's version of the family tree which traces the ancestry of Jesus back to David and Abraham, thus making Jesus heir of the promises to the royal house and to the chosen people, or Luke's genealogy

27

which works backwards through these figures to Adam himself, the first son of God. The Church celebrates Jesus as so much one of us that we can take delight in spelling out the generation after generation that produced him, singing of all those men and women with their failures and downright wickedness who make up the family tree of Jesus. For Jesus does not come of a particularly good family. His family is in fact particularly ungood for much of its past. In the *Te Deum* we sing to Christ *Non horruisti virginis uterum*: 'You did not scorn the Virgin's womb.' At first sight that seems rather strange language to use about the Virgin in the Catholic tradition where she is honoured as Mary Immaculate. But surely it is Mary's questionable parentage which is in debate here. The hymn celebrates the extraordinary condescension of Jesus in being prepared to take not the flesh of Adam before the Fall but the flesh of all those generations stretching from Adam through Abraham and David down to Mary. The *Te Deum* is out to praise that unlooked-for mercy of his, whereby he was prepared to become a descendant of people even like King Manasseh of whom the Bible can find nothing good to say. We solemnly sing that fact, rejoicing in it and surrounding it with the wealth of ceremonial, just as gladly as we sing the *Exsultet* of Easter. And why not? If there were no such family tree, what would there be for us especially, as the people we are, to exult over in the message of Easter? But because he does have such a genealogy we can pray to him with confidence.

So we pray to him: 'O Root of Jesse'. This means praying to him as Son of David, as son of all those kings after David, people like Solomon and Asa and Manasseh and Jeconiah. If he was prepared to come to an Israel and a world that had produced people like that, then we can fairly expect that he will be prepared to come to our world and our hearts with all their accumulated weight of wickedness. We can be confident that he will come to us as we are, coming through our past and making it his own. In this way he will reach us where we are and transform our past so that when we tell the story of our lives we will be able to include gladly in that story all the mistakes we have made and all the blind alleys we have explored. Not that we cease to regret. Not that we excuse ourselves for our mistakes and wrong turnings. Not that we become complacent about our evil deeds and thoughts and words. It is not as though what was once bad has now become good, as if Manasseh were to be the Messiah. But if and when Messiah comes to us, then we can sing the story of our lives as the story of the path which

Messiah took to come to us, leaping upon the mountains and bounding over the hills as the Fathers say in quotation from the Song of Songs. When Messiah comes we can tell the story of our past all over again, as nations retell their history after a change in their fortunes, as Israel learned to tell the story of her past as the story of God's graciousness. It is a mistake to brood over our past. It is a misunderstanding of what Messiah means for us to worry about our past. That past which has slipped away from us, out of our power to control, is only the raw materials of a story. What matters is how we tell the story using those raw materials. If Messiah has indeed come, then the story can be solemnly and gladly sung, to the accompaniment of all that makes for rejoicing.

The *Radix* of the Latin antiphon is both root and shoot. 'There shall come forth a shoot from the stump of Jesse.'[28] This 'shoot' is the novelty that springs up from the past, the newness that the tradition produces. Literally, the most radical man is the man who is well-rooted, who has got back to his roots. We are to be well-rooted in our individual past, with a sense of where we have come from, of what we were and started out with, and of where we have been since we first started out. Similarly, we must be well-rooted in our collective and communal past. If we are ever going to be radicals in the way in which the Root of Jesse is radical, productive of new and unexpected growth, shooting up with fresh life and vigour, then we must be rooted in our tradition. Again and again it has proved to be the case that the more firmly the Church or some group within the Church is rooted in its past, the more vigorously it can produce new growth. There is a kind of traditionalism that is really dead, for it consists in simply repeating the time-hallowed (or perhaps one should say time-desecrated) formulae and styles of doing things. But there is also a kind of traditionalism that is altogether necessary for any real renewal. If we want to renew our lives together then at least some of us must be thoroughly steeped in our tradition with an intimate and interior acquaintance. In particular, some of us at least must know the way things were at the beginning, the landmarks our fathers in faith, or in a religious family in the Church, set up for us. But if only some of us need to read and go on reading the source material of our tradition and be able to communicate it to others, all of us without exception must have a sense of what our tap-roots are, of how fresh it all was once, of how relative our sense of staleness is and how it is possible for it all to be fresh again, since the root can still shoot. For it *can* shoot again. The tree of Adam can become the tree of Christ's cross. The tree which was once the tree of life and became the tree of death for so many people can always be the tree of life again for us, as it has always been for so many of those who have gone before us in the Church and in our communities. As the legends say, it is the same tree. There is no reason why it should not shoot and be green again in us.

O Clavis David: 20 December

O Key of David, and sceptre of the house of Israel, you open and no man can shut, you shut and no man can open: come and bring bound out of the dungeon him who is sitting in darkness and in the shadow of death.

In the *O Radix* we prayed for Christ to come and to deliver us. This style of praying which involves the apparent absurdity of giving orders to God, is met with time and again in the psalms. It springs from what the New Testament calls *parrhesia*, the boldness to come before the Lord and say anything to him you like. Not anything that comes into our heads, however, but anything that comes out of our hearts. There is not much point in merely chattering at God, filling the air with verbal pollution. But what comes out of the abundance of our hearts can and should be brought to God. When we 'have our hearts within', as Gregory the Great puts it, there will be times when we have to say things to God which go beyond the limits of polite speech. Like Job complaining about God and to God we pray, 'Come to deliver us and to set us free!' This passion for freedom is the hallmark of the Jewish–Christian tradition: freedom from Egypt and from the iron furnace, freedom from the tyranny of that most cruel Pharoah, the Devil, freedom from sin, from death and from hell.

But this passion for freedom presupposes a sense of not being free at the moment. We would not pray so insistently to the Root of David to come to set us free unless we knew that we were held bound in some sort of prison. We are free in faith surely, but not yet sure that we have given ourselves so completely to God that we are free with the freedom which, in principle, he has given us. We still have a sense of frustration, of not being able to do what we want to do. But real freedom never consists in an unlimited exercise of free choice. Real freedom means, rather, being able to do exactly

31

what we want to do, because we want all that God wants and only what God wants. It is because we are frustrated even in our good ambitions that we pray the Lord to come and lead us out of the prison-house where we are limited and circumscribed against our will. The Latin text of the antiphon seems to imply, interestingly enough, that God can lead us out from where we are sitting in darkness precisely by leading us out bound, bound now to him. Paradoxically, our liberation takes the form of slavery where we find ourselves enthralled, spell-bound, captivated by his presence. What we want is not to be a law unto ourselves but to belong only to Christ. In belonging to him alone will we be ourselves and find freedom. If Christ is going to make his way into our prison-house and lead us out from it, then he will need at times to use his own kind of force, in order to compel us to come in. This is what John Donne saw:

> Batter my heart, three personed God, for you
> as yet but knock, breathe, shine and seek to mend;
> that I may rise and stand, o'erthrow me, and bend
> your force to break, blow, burn and make me new.
> I, like an usurped town, to another due,
> labour to admit you, but O to no end.
> Reason, your viceroy in me, me should defend,
> but is captived and proves weak or untrue.
> Yet dearly I love you, and would be loved fain,
> but as betrothed unto your enemy.
> Divorce me, untie me, or break that knot again,
> Take me to you, imprison me, for I
> except you enthral me, never shall be free,
> nor ever chaste, except you ravish me.[29]

This prison house from which we seek to be delivered is not, of course, the body, the flesh and blood that Jesus now shares with us for ever. It is not the material world, which we seek not to be delivered from but to see transfigured. It is the devouring element, what the Roman Liturgy calls the 'lion's mouth', Tartarus, which would swallow us up if it had the chance. In one sense we can identify this element with the so-called 'real world', the world which psychiatrists and social scientists and tycoons in advertising firms want us to adjust to and be at home in. That world saps our integrity and eats up our whole personality, giving us not freedom

32

to do what we really want to do but a whole set of false wants and artificial and quite unnecessary 'needs'. There seems to be nothing that could be invented but not sold, no gadget on which its inventor could not make a packet. From this system of false wants and falsely conceived needs we pray the Key of David to come and deliver us. We ask him to ravish us so that we may be chaste from those inordinate desires which other people artificially produce in us. Poverty of spirit, not having artificial desires, is of a piece with chastity, which involves not having perverted desires.

But the prison-house which ultimately holds people bound is the house of death itself, that realm which takes hold of us while we are still alive and which we begin to experience in all the frustration that we experience now. Hell, the kingdom of death, is but the logic of our present situation insofar as that situation is unredeemed. Hell does not strictly await a man, but is created by his arrival. So it is not so much the due punishment of our present as our present unredeemed being taken to its logical conclusion and seen in its pure form, if the word 'pure' may be allowed here. To this hell, as we affirm in the Creed, Christ himself goes. We do not just pray to him to take us out of problematic situations and particular places where we find ourselves unfree. We ask him to set us free from the ultimate possibilities of our unfreedom, from death itself. Here we pray in fellowship with the patriarchs and prophets of Israel, with all those kings who desired to see what we have seen but never saw it, and to hear what we have heard but never heard it. In their lifetime there was always hope; until they died there was always that possibility that Messiah would come. But at their death they were fixed like flies in amber in the moment of the frustration of their deepest desires. In them, as we pray with them, we can see ourselves. We pray to the Key of David to come, therefore, and to lead out the one man who is the human race, who is all of us bound together in one bundle of life.

'Come and deliver us from hell,' we say, from the pointlessness and meaninglessness of it all, the logic that holds us trapped. If we can pray, then we can hope. If we can pray, then we are in the hell of the patriarchs that was full of hope, not Dante's hell which was full of despair. If we can pray, then there is a chance that something radically new will happen to us. For in the hell of the patriarchs people still live in time. They cry out to the Lord to delay no longer, that it is time to have mercy on Zion, that the time has come. Living thus in time, they let their past die. They do not go on and

33

on living in their past, but they tell the story of it as past, a past from which God has promised to deliver them and *will* deliver them in his own good time.

'Come, O Key of David.' The Christ of the Apocalypse has the Key of David, as the conqueror of a city was presented with the keys of the city gate, and here he is personally that key. The conqueror is the Christ who was dead; but look, he is alive for evermore. He is the key that opens the door on to a new creation and a new age. He opens the future to us, releasing us from the gloom of our own logic through the power of the keys. It is within this sort of perspective that we can see the significance of that sacrament we usually associate with the keys, confession, the sacrament of post-baptismal repentance. We are always more or less liable to get ourselves stuck in our past. We tend not to let the record play on but to get it caught, so that the same trivial bit of the tune goes on repeating itself again and again. It's all so dull. That dullness is one of the worst features of sin, the typical dreariness of the shadow of death. The keys are there to lead us out from that prison house of our own past, out of our habitual ways of thinking and feeling, away from all that dreariness into new possibilities where our feet are set at large. What we do in making our confession is to acknowledge that we are pretty dull people, in this sense. There is never any need to try to make life exciting for the priest by representing our sins as different from those of other people, or even from the sins of last time. You can fairly expect your little list to be rather dreary: even the whoppers are as stale as yesterday's newspapers. That is built into the nature, or rather the un-nature, of sin. In confession we pray to the Key of David to come and lead us out from all this, to bind us with his love and loose us from other loves. And always we experience to some extent (no matter how small an extent) that we are led out, our feet set at large for a while (no matter how small a while). Again and again we will go back to our pettiness and dreariness, but never back to quite the pettiness and dreariness that we had before. We will never fail in quite the same way, because then was then and now is now. And if we can let the past be dead, let time go on and be real time, then we can begin to acquire a sense of a time when something radically new will indeed happen. A time when the Key of David will turn in the lock and release us from the dreariness of it all into the dawn, the new day of the Resurrection.

'Come, Key of David', we sing on 20 December. In the Middle

34

Ages they used to sing this antiphon at other times as well. In particular, they used to sing it when a recluse entered his cell or anchorhold, built alongside the parish church, perhaps, or by some monastery wall. As the recluse was walled up the bishop would lead the people in invoking the Key of David, praying that Christ might shut the door on the recluse in such a way that no man would be able to open it, but also to open doors before him so wide that no man would be able to shut them. The recluse was cloistered in the strictest possible sense so that he might walk at liberty before God. He entered, in as symbolically literal a way as possible, into the experience of the Lord on Holy Saturday, going down alive into Hell, free amongst the dead, so as to help Christ harrow hell. His life was hidden with Christ in God, making visible in the walls of his anchorhold the hiddenness in God of every life that is lived with Christ. A life that is Holy Saturday is a very active life, a life engaged in the warfare against the demons. What those demons are and how potent they are, we shall never know until we go down into hell. 'Keep your mind in hell and despair not',[30] as a modern Russian monk was told. Our wrestling is not against flesh and blood, it is not just problems on the sociological level, about time-tables and inter-personal relationships. Our wrestling is 'against the spiritual hosts of wickedness',[31] against demons whose very existence we had never suspected until we entered some sort of enclosure of our bodies so that our minds might be free to serve him. Certainly, any kind of religious life worth the name must have some element of Holy Saturday about it. What have we to give to God except ourselves? And how do we give anything at all to God except by letting him give what he wants to us? And what does he wish to give us except that freedom for which Christ has set us free, the freedom which we taste in battling with him against the demons of our life-long cloister. The demand that makes on us, in terms of poverty and the simplification of life, is that we should have no armour, no defence, save the shield of faith and the helmet of salvation, and the sword of the Spirit, which is the Word of God.

O Oriens: 21 December

For these Advent antiphons that we are taking as our texts for meditation, what more than anything else seems to mark out the unredeemed aspect of our lives is darkness and the shadow of death. Our darkness is a prison: yesterday we asked the Key of David to come and open the prison doors. Today we say that we are imprisoned in darkness: so we ask the Dayspring, the brightness of eternal light, the sun of righteousness, to come and shine on us.

O Rising Sun, you are the splendour of eternal light and the sun of justice. O come and enlighten those who sit in darkness and in the shadow of death.

The trouble with darkness is that nothing appears for what it really is. Everything gets out of proportion. We lose our sense of direction and our feeling for whether things are near or distant, and indeed our capacity to judge what a thing is, a bush or a highwayman, a stick or a snake on the ground before us. There may be other people sitting in the dark with us but in darkness we have little contact with them. We may hold hands and whistle to keep up our courage, but we cannot see the expression on the other's face. We have no more than his voice to go on, such is the isolation of the darkness where we are sitting. The dark may give us ersatz emotions and disproportionate reactions to sounds, so that we are falsely frightened or falsely relieved. It is appropriate that the theatre of illusion should normally require its audience to sit in darkness, so that they can be transported into an unreal world where they forget one another and look only at the unreality of what is presented from outside. And so we pray for light: *O Oriens!* If light is a well-nigh universal symbol for divinity, the element proper to God or the gods, what is proper to Christ our Lord is the *new* light, the dawn, the light of the east, the light of the sun at its

36

rising. Before it was known that 'Jesus' would be the name of the Christ, it was known that the Messiah would be the Dawn, the Orient, the Rising Day, for he would be newness and novelty. 'Behold I will bring my Servant, the Orient, the Dawn,'[32] God says through the prophet Zechariah; 'Behold the man whose name is the Orient, the Rising Day, for he shall rise up in his place, and he shall build the temple of the Lord.'[33] And when the immediate forerunner of Jesus was born, another Zechariah was filled with the Holy Spirit and prophesied saying: 'Through the loving kindness of the heart of our God, the Dayspring shall visit us from on high, to give light to those who sit in darkness and in the shadow of death, to guide our feet into the way of peace.'[34]

Day by day, dawn by dawn, we take up those words of the father of John the Baptist and we sing them with him in the canticle of Lauds, the *Benedictus*. It is a canticle with a strange and intricate structure of words and phrases, weaving in and out with the pattern of a dance. The message of this chant is not openly declared in the words themselves, for it lies hidden also in the way the words are used, in their positioning. This is all of a piece with how St Luke, in whose gospel the *Benedictus* appears, sees human history, not as just a succession of events but, rather, a meaningful pattern which he invites us to enter. In St Luke's pattern our present situation is the fulfilment of the promises of the past but in its turn it carries the promise of the future. The promises of the Old Testament have been fulfilled in us who live in the time of Christ. Therefore we trust that the promises of our own time will be fulfilled in their turn in the time of Christ's Advent, when the Kingdom of God finally comes in power. We are shepherds and guardians of the future as well as recipients of the fulfilled promises of the past. All that is figured in the *Benedictus*. Each morning we are invited to see the sun that is rising over our world that day as a pledge of the reality of the Sun that rose the first Easter morning, rose after he had set in blood, after he had been down in the depths of the earth. This day which is just beginning is a day when the resurrection of Jesus can be lived out in our lives. But this rising day is itself the pledge, promise and prophecy of the Dawn that will rise over the world on the day of the great and general resurrection, the Dawn of that Day that will never end. Today we can live risen lives that will be pledges of the life we shall lead in that first Day which will be an eternal Day. We should live our lives quite consciously between this past and this future, and in the light of this Day which is rising to

37

give light to those who have been sitting in darkness. And that means to all those who find life obscure, who cannot get things into proportion. It means those who have been afraid where no fear was, who have been unsure whether what they dimly sensed near them was tame or horrific.

We have to live, then, in a real continuity with the past, trying to be so at home there that we make it contemporary with us. Our relationship with the past, with the traditional life of the Church, will give us a sense of due proportion and perspective. But equally we must live as guardians of the future, living towards that future which will be the Resurrection but also towards the future that will be in ten years' or in fifty years' time. That involves trying to acquire a sense of where the world and where the church is going, not trying to manufacture the future – which should be left to the creative hand of God – but trying to see how the God who is always true to himself is shaping our world now. It is rather like watching a sculptor working on a piece of stone. We can get a sense, long before the statue is finished, of what it is going to be. To change the metaphor, we can look in the direction to which various lines are pointing and be obedient to the future on which they converge. This may involve being prepared to change a number of things in the way we have been living to date, turning them round to face the dawn. (In all this, professional religious and the middle-aged should be the two sets of people most ready to change, for they should have a sense of what matters and what does not.) We have to live with a sense of responsibility towards the past which prophesied us, and towards the future we carry within us. But we have to live *today*, in the day that is dawning now. The pattern of the incarnation is that we should be all there in all of our activities, reading when we read, recreating when we recreate, praying when we pray. God is to be found not by abstracting ourselves from our ordinary tasks but by looking at what we are involved with in depth. So it was that the eternal God was seen not by abstracting the Palestinian Jew from the flesh and blood of Jesus but by looking directly at him. Whoever has seen him, in all his historical particularity, has seen the Father.

If we are ever to move towards that future which we are promised, the best way of moving from the place where we are now is to open our sails and let the wind of the Holy Spirit come and blow us some place else. If the way Christian righteousness exceeded that of the scribes and pharisees were by there being more things for us to do and to avoid, that would not be very much of a gospel, a good news. But before Jesus is a lawgiver he is, as we say, the Sun of righteousness itself. He is the one of whom Malachi prophesied: 'Unto you that fear my name shall the sun of righteousness arise with healing in his wings'.[35] Wings, because the sun seems to fly through the heavens like a great bird; wings, as the sun-disk is winged in Egyptian monuments. The light that the rising sun of the day of Adonai brings is a light that heals, opening the eyes of the blind. He brings healing just because he is the very justice of God. God's justice is not God conforming himself to some eternal standard of justice but a reality that God creates by adjusting us to himself and to each other. Our righteousness exceeds that of the scribes and pharisees only in that we accept such 'justification', the way God has done things for us and for other people.

O Rex Gentium: 22 December

Today we pray:

> O King whom all the peoples desire, you are the corner-stone
> which makes all one, O come and save man whom you made
> from clay.

King whom all the peoples desire! It was not only patriarchs and
prophets who were waiting in the land of the shades. It was not
only to patriarchs and prophets, to the men of Israel, that the Light
went when it went down into hell, down like Orpheus into the
underworld to rescue Eurydice. That hell was the place of all the
dead, where all men were in the same condition. It was the place
where the most significant division in the world – between Israel,
the one people that was chosen, and the very many peoples who
were not – was no longer of any significance. It was not only the
prophets and kings of Israel who failed to hear and see the object
of all their longing. What they longed for was perhaps clearer to
them than to many of the others, in that so often they already
realized that what they were wanting and waiting for was in fact a
Who, a person, the One who would be sent. And they had faith in
the Messiah who was to come, and in that way were already saved.
But there were countless numbers of the unchosen who, without
any such clear expectations, hoped nevertheless for a change in
their fortunes, for a new golden age to come on the world. We
belong with them, for we are their sons according to the flesh, even
though we may be the sons of Abraham and Isaac and Jacob
according to the spirit. We must not sever our bond of union with
them but on the contrary remember our kinship and cultivate our
piety towards our own forebears. And so we pray: *O Rex gentium, et
Desideratus earum*: 'O king of the gentiles, you whom the gentiles so
desire.' He was and is desired not only by his first love, the chosen

people, but by the peoples who were not elected but who, for all that, are not outside his love.

In so praying, we give voice to the desire of the world for something or someone to change its situation, to make the world a better place. We pray for some sort of figure who will take responsibility for our future well-being. That desire, however, can be only impotent if our wish is to be allowed to shirk and shrug off responsibility for ourselves and for one another. We need to purify our desires from that. We are not praying for a *führer*, but for the king who makes his people a nation of kings. If we pray him to come, then we must be ready to share his kingship. Those who, according to the *Apocalypse* of St John, will sit with him on his throne are those who have conquered as he has conquered; they are those whom he has freed from their sins by his blood, and made a kingdom, priests to his God and Father. Christ is King, surely, but he is not a king whose royalty is diminished by sharing it with other people. Again and again we tend to think that if God shares things with us, he will be lessened by it, but that is not so. Christ is none the less a priest but all the more a priest in that he makes all of us priests too. God is none the less holy but the more holy in that he makes us really holy as well. God is all the more God, all the more other, in that he makes us sharers in his very nature as God, as Peter in his second epistle and the church fathers insist. So when we pray for him to come as King we are not asking for a sugar-daddy to relieve us of all responsibility for our world. We are praying for a king who will restore us to our rightful position as kings in the world he has made, for, as the Roman Liturgy puts it, we are 'set over the whole world to serve him, our Creator, and to rule over all creatures'.[36]

The King of the gentiles makes us kings in turn; we whom he formed *de limo*, out of the dust and slime of the earth. The *Genesis* myth speaks of God forming man from the mist-watered earth, and of his breathing into man's nostrils the breath of life so that man became a living being, or a 'speaking spirit' as the Jewish Targum on the passage puts it. We cannot speak of the young earth save in the language of fairy tales. But it is we ourselves who are involved in that story, created from the dust, confronted by God and the will of God, addressed by him, accused by him in the story of Adam's fall, sentenced and expelled by him, and cared for by him even in our wanderings far from Eden. In that mythical story we are all at stake. We are reminded of that every year at the start of that other

41

purple season of Lent, when the Church says to us on Ash Wednes-day: 'Remember, man, that you are dust and that to dust you will return.' Remember the reality of the situation. There is nothing special about you. How long it takes for us to recognize that, just as it takes a long time for most of us to realize, on the existential level, that we are mortal. Not only in Lent but throughout the entire year and perhaps especially today as we repeat this antiphon, we stand, each one of us, under the sign of the ashes, the dust of the earth. That is the sign of our solidarity in human nature and fallen nature. It is also the sign of our solidarity in the Lamb of God who takes away the sin of the world, the risen Lord, the King who is to come and whom the gentiles so desire.

He, we say, is the Cornerstone that makes both peoples one, forging a unity out of Jew and gentile. According to Paul, this is the heart of the mystery that was hidden from before all ages but has now been revealed. The mystery of the Church as the sign and instrument of unity between men. The mystery of the gospel that is spoken to men who do not speak each other's languages so that they may with one heart and one mouth confess the faith of Christ. The whole object of the exercise in Christ's coming is that he should gather together into one the children of God who are scattered abroad. Therefore we must always have something of his concern for unity, in mankind and, most particularly, in the Church. We must have a care for the unity of the great Church, and for the unity of our local churches, those churches which are smaller in numbers and geographical extent than the *catholica* but which are just as much Church as she is. Our aim should be not just to preserve a quiet life, but to go out of our way to *make* peace. That is where the beatitude lies, in the making of the peace it speaks of. And peace is made by the cross. It is made by our suffering, as much as our activity. It is made by our refusing to return hostility, by the gentle answer that turns away wrath. It is made by being prepared to waive our rights and to give up our pet scheme where nothing more is at stake in them than our own interests and where the common good, the peace of the brotherhood, is at stake on the other side. The peace we share comes from the readiness of Jesus to forego his peace, to die rather than to destroy the peace that God had prepared for us. The peace we share is the peace that flows from the death of Jesus, the peace of the covenant in the blood of Christ that was shed by violence.

O Immanuel: 23 December

For days and days now we have put ourselves with those patriarchs and prophets who for long centuries desired to see and hear what was neither seen nor heard until that night in the cave at Bethlehem, that night in which the hopes and fears of all the years were gathered together in royal David's city. We have sat with them in darkness and in the shadow of death, in the recognition of our common humanity. We like they are formed from the dust of the earth, and we shall return to dust exactly as they have. We have remembered as they remembered how the Lord appeared to Moses in the burning bush and gave him the Law of Sinai. And now, taught to hope by Isaiah, we pray to the one whom he prophesied. We call out:

> O Immanuel, you are our king and our judge, the One whom the peoples await and their Saviour. O come and save us, Lord, our God.

The Virgin shall conceive and bear a son and shall call his name Immanuel, God-with-us. If we are really going to be saved, it can be by none other than God himself. The patriarchs and prophets had always known that, even though they never guessed that God himself would become altogether one of us and never imagined that he would be 'with us' in such an astonishing and paradoxical fashion. Yet how could the Saviour God not be Immanuel when the first time that Israel had been saved it had been the Lord himself who had done it? Year by year, as the story of the Exodus from Egypt was recounted at Passover they would come to the verse 'And the Lord brought us out of Egypt'. On this text the gloss ran: 'Not by any intermediary, not by any seraph, not by any messenger, but God himself in his glory, the Holy One, blessed be he'.[37] The second deliverance could not be any less marvellous than the first, that exodus from Egypt's land. So they prayed for Immanuel to

43

come, even though it was not a man they longed to see, nor human accents they longed to hear.

When we pray for Immanuel to come, we pray as people who know how God is with us so much that he is one of us. We pray knowing the wonder of it all, knowing that he has already come in such a way that there is no going back on that coming. He has become man so as never more to be unmanned. So much of the prophesy is already fulfilled. The Virgin Israel in the person of the Virgin Mary has brought forth her Son. She will never bring him forth in that way again. History is irreversible. There can be no question of Jesus being born a second time in the way he was born in Bethlehem, just as there can be no question of his being killed a second time as he was killed on Calvary. From now on for all eternity there is a man on the throne of God, a man nearest to the Father's heart. The incarnation is not reversible by any eventuality. And so his coming *to be* Immanuel is not something that we can pray for now; we can pray to him *as* Immanuel, but not pray for him to become Immanuel. The fact that he is Immanuel is not something to pray for but to rejoice in. Above all we rejoice in it in the Holy Eucharist, the Blessed Sacrament. In the Mass we plead Christ's death before the Father, acknowledging his resurrection and awaiting his return. But for centuries in the Church there has been the custom of reserving the Blessed Sacrament outside of the Mass, not simply for the purpose of giving communion to the sick and dying but for its own sake. The Blessed Sacrament is there so that we may rejoice in the presence of the Lord amongst us for its own sake. He is glad to be amongst us, eternal Wisdom delighting to dwell with the sons of men, the Word that was made flesh and tabernacled amongst us. Prayer before the Blessed Sacrament should be primarily the prayer of rejoicing, of saying how good it is for us to be there. His presence is the summing up of all the mighty works of God for us and for our salvation. In the sacred mysteries of his body and blood is the memorial of all the great acts of God in the past. We can sing psalms of thanksgiving for them as we sing in delight of the eucharistic presence. 'He gives bread to all living things', wrote the psalmist, 'great is his love, love without end.'[38] Little did the sweet singer of Israel guess what that bread would be, and how he would give the true and living Bread, the body of eternal Wisdom, the Sun of Righteousness, Immanuel. But we, knowing what that Bread is, can rejoice in the real presence of all his mighty works summed up in the most mighty work of his

44

love, the incarnation of his Word. And then, when we have rejoiced, we can surely pray for the needs of the world to the God and Father of us all, asking him to bring in his Kingdom in its fulness. There, in the presence of him who will come in glory to both King and Kingdom, we can pray the Father to be true to himself and to complete his work for us men and for our salvation. Or, to put it another way, we can pray to Immanuel to come and answer all our longings.

We pray to Immanuel who is our King, the King who makes us kings. But the antiphons get more intimate and more insistent, as befits our praying to someone who is one of ourselves. 'Our king and our judge . . . come and save us!' There is a paradox in this, because the way our King will save us is by coming and giving us more of his law as our Judge. St Thomas puts the question as to the identity of this new law of Christ. And he replies that it can only be the grace of the Spirit himself. What the Lord demands of us he gives us. The love of God, the love which God has for us, has been shed abroad in our hearts by the Holy Spirit who has been given us. We will know what the love Jesus commands at the Last Supper is like when we learn how to let the Lord love in us. We shall find that out when we abandon our attempts to force ourselves to love other people and instead let the Lord love them through us by pouring the Holy Spirit, the law of the New Testament into our hearts. Immanuel as man, as our King, has more to teach us than he did when he was on Sinai's height. Nothing is good unless it is first prudent, but prudence takes wings when the way of prudence is taught us no longer by Eternal Wisdom in some distant heaven but by Eternal Wisdom now made man, Immanuel. Prudence becomes very different when it is taken over by the Holy Spirit himself. There is a prudence which comes from God and transforms our natural prudence without making us plain silly. Many considerations would not occur to us without the inspiration of the Holy Spirit. Wisdom and understanding, counsel and fortitude, knowledge and devotion and the fear of the Lord, these are the gifts poured out by the Spirit, though in different measure, upon all Christians. Those gifts, so much more important than the charisms about which we hear so much nowadays, are said to be necessary for our salvation. The righteousness of the scribes and pharisees, the behaviour of the ordinary decent man and the ordinary decent churchgoer will not suffice to save us, but only the Holy Spirit in his gifts. To come to God requires some degree of passivity, of opening the sails to let the mighty, rushing wind which is the Holy Spirit, blow us where it will. We have to be ready for a degree of unpredictability in ourselves and in our communities – although this is not the same as going random. Without a readiness to spread our sails and catch the wind of the Holy Spirit we will not make harbour, quite apart from not having the fun of all the yachting on the open sea before we do. We shall lose out if we miss that yachting on the Sea Pacific over whose surface the dove hovers and the mighty rushing wind of the Spirit blows.

'O Immanuel, come and save us.' We ourselves as we really are now. Not where we were a while ago, at our baptism, or our first communion, or during the fervour of our novitiate or when we took solemn vows. Be Immanuel just where we are. Not where we will be when we have rid ourselves of that terrible bad habit we cannot shake off, nor where we will be when we have managed to love this dreadfully bothersome brother a little bit more, nor where we will be at the moment of our death, surrounded and fortified by all the rites of Holy Church. Be where we are now. And here what we need to do, in the last analysis, is not to pray that he will be where we are, but to understand that he already is where we are. When we really grasp that he has found us, that he is where we are, then we can go and seek him. He is the Glory of God who sat with the exiles by the waters of Babylon and wept with them in the night. Where we sit now is a good enough place for Immanuel to come and to enlighten us.

Christmas Eve

In the Christmas Liturgy we make a memorial of the way in which the Messiah who was desired, albeit inarticulately, by all nations did come to all nations and for all nations. On Christmas Eve in the old liturgy there took place a solemn chapter, which all the brethren were strictly bound to attend. The chapter room, says our Dominican *Caeremoniale*, is fittingly adorned with hangings and lights. The lectern is surrounded with flowers and richly veiled. The brethren stand for the reading of the Martyrology, the book which each day tells you the feasts which are being celebrated that day in all the different churches of the world – in theory, at least. Today, instead of monotoning the Martyrology, the cantor sings it. When he reaches the key section of it he raises his voice a full fifth and sings the crucial words, the good news of Christmas, *solemniter ac morosius*, solemnly and with dignity. When he tells us how the eternal Son of the eternal Father was made man, all the brethren prostrate themselves and pray in silence for a while. Then they sit down and listen to the rest of the Martyrology, to the account of the lives and deaths of those Christians who were born into heaven on the day in which Christ was born on earth. After the Martyrology, according to the tradition of the English Province, the youngest novice preaches a Latin sermon, asking a blessing beforehand in his efforts, and making the *venia*, or ritual kissing of the scapular and prostration, when he has finished, in recognition of his temerity in speaking before the grave fathers. Then the prior is supposed to say a few words inviting the brethen to the celebration of so great a solemnity. The chapter closes with a general absolution so that nothing may hinder the joy of the feast.

Nowadays, this traditional chapter business has been spread around the day, so that the general absolution and the sermon (Latin or otherwise!) comes during the Mass of Christmas Eve, and the Martyrology itself is read in the Vigil that ends with the Mass of Christmas Night. 'O come, o come, Emmanuel', we sing at the beginning of the Vigil, for the last calling out from our Advent. And in answer to our call we hear the words of the Martyrology telling us how he did come and save us.

> Be comforted, be comforted, my people, says your God. For in the year 5199 from the creation of the world, when in the beginning God created heaven and earth, in the year 2957 from the flood, in the year 2015 from the birth of Abraham, in the year 1510 from Moses and the going forth of the people of Israel from Egypt, in the year 1032 from the anointing of David as king, in the sixty-fifth week according to the prophecy of Daniel. . . .

So far, all of this is very Jewish, although even here there is a proclamation of significance for more than simply Israel. Israel's meaning is not Israel: it is all mankind. Abraham was chosen so that in him all the nations of the earth might be blessed. He was chosen for the sake of the heavens and the earth which God created, and for the sake of those seven people who were in the ark with Noah, the mystic eight from whose loins, in Jewish tradition, the seventy nations of man were formed. What the Martyrology is about to announce to us affects all of that. Jesus gives signficance to the birth of Abraham, and to Moses and to David, who are themselves the meaning of the Flood and the Creation. The text continues:

> In the one hundred and ninety-fourth Olympiad, in the year 752 from the foundation of the city of Rome, in the forty-second year of the reign of Octavian Augustus.

An olympiad is the length of time which elapsed between one set of games at Olympus and the next, and the succession of olympiads has served to fix the time of many momentous events. Before it, history at least in the West was an almost entirely fabulous and once-upon-a-time affair. So Jewish and Greek methods of computing time are presented together, for in Christ, whom the Martyrology proclaims, there is neither Jew nor Greek. Roman methods follow, for all are one, are one man, in him. 'In the forty-second year of the reign of Octavian Augustus . . . in the sixth age of the world . . .' History is periodized here into different world epochs, just as we do ourselves. We speak of the Classical era, the early, high and late Middle Ages, the Renaissance, modern and contemporary history and so forth. In Jewish and Christian tradition as age differs from age so does the relationship between God and man. What is appropriate in one age is not appropriate in the next. The covenant after the Flood with Noah was superseded, though not replaced, by the covenant God made with Abraham, which in its turn gave way to the covenant of Sinai, itself further elucidated by the covenant with David. And finally, there was the promise of a new and definitive covenant. In this way of thinking, your life should follow the covenant in whose age you live. Taking our cue from patristic insights, we should see these ages or epochs or covenants as very far from monolithic. To take a secular analogue, it does not make sense for us to speak of a mask carved in the Niger Delta in 1420 as 'medieval'. The Middle Ages were the Western European Middle Ages. Different cultures have different epochs. The epochs to which the Martyrology alludes are not just epochs that Israel has experienced. They are, for the most part, ages to which different contemporary cultures may still belong. The covenant with Noah, for example, is seen in both Jewish and patristic Christian writing as a covenant which still applies to the greater part of the world. Only when a new covenant is offered does an old one become obsolete and, even, lethal. In the lives of cultures, and even in our individual lives, certain styles of behaviour may be tolerable at one stage and eventually become unacceptable and wrong at another. For all of us there are liable to be fairly pre-Christian elements within us, elements in our personalities on which we cannot, at the moment, make Christian demands. Certainly, they must have the good news preached to them and be transformed, but not until the right time comes for them to be able to receive it. And epochs, ages, covenant times are finally the choice of God, who disposes of all times and all seasons. This is what the Martyrology is saying. The times and seasons are in the hand of God. He disposes of them as he knows best, making all things work together for good.

'In the sixth age of the world, when all the world was at peace.' This seems to be a genuine historical reminiscence. At the time of the birth of Jesus the whole Roman world was at peace. For the first and last time the gates of the temple of Mars in the Forum Romanum were closed. How appropriate it was, say the fathers, that when all the world was at peace the Prince of Peace was born. For the sake of his coming the world had been brought for a while to peace. Again, it is the idea of eternal Wisdom ordering all things mightily and gently. From that cosmic scale we are invited to draw the pattern of God's working in our individual lives, how he mightily and gently orders all things for our good.

For at that time,

> when the whole world was at peace, Jesus Christ, eternal God and Son of the eternal Father, willing to hallow the world by his most gracious coming, having been conceived by the Holy Spirit, and nine months having passed since his conception, was born in Bethlehem of Juda, made man of the Virgin Mary.

To hallow the world – that is always why he wants to come, to make holy, to make over for God, to bring to a goal and conclusion, to make of reality what it was made to be. His most gracious coming, *piissimo*, most merciful, gentle, loving, even dutiful, perhaps. Jesus' coming is motivated by love, mercy and respect for us whom he makes his ancestors and brothers. Here, as the name of Jesus is first mentioned, the cantor raises his voice, and at the end of the clause everyone falls to the ground in the gesture of *proskunesis*, like the Magi before the child Jesus. We make the same gesture on Good Friday when the death of Jesus is rehearsed in the passion story. Before the mysteries of the birth and death of the Word what else is there for us to do other than to fall down and keep silence for a while? This silence is not the kind of ascetic silence that makes a guru out of the environment around us: it is, rather, that variety of silence which is laid upon us by the sheer marvel of the thing. Christians, and especially Dominicans, have to say things about God and what belongs to God: they have to make words of the Word. But our first response must be the silence of being so overwhelmed by the wonder of it all that we feel there is nothing we could possibly say. Words worth anything will normally be born out of that silence. As, according to Ignatius of Antioch, the Word himself proceeds out of silence, so our words which embody him will often and most typically proceed from the silence that his most merciful coming produces. There is nothing to feel worried about if you find it hard to make words of the Word, so that you must tease and coax them out of your silence before God and the things of God. It would be much more worrying if you were always shouting your mouth off about the great mysteries of the faith, always trying to master them and control the access of others to them, rather than trying to stand with other people before the mystery and to lead them to share your silence. Perhaps we never see in a more ideogrammatic way what being a Dominican is all about than when together and with the people of God at large we fall down in silence before the *mysterium tremendum et fascinans* of the God who is born and the God who dies, when we have made a space of silence in which we can be with the whole Church in the presence of the mighty works of God.

And then, at the end of all that dating and theology and of that profound silence the cantor sings, 'The birth of our Lord Jesus Christ according to the flesh'. Israel, Greece, Rome and the world at large are thus situated by reference to the birth of Jesus according to the flesh. This is a pretty startling claim, one which we may feel some embarrassment in making. Is it not too much of a piece with treating theology as the queen of the sciences, the belief that theology might receive the findings of all other disciplines and knit them together in an organic whole? To modern people it seems obvious that every discipline must be allowed its full autonomy; we expect our universities to be open, free and liberal, pluralist and non-confessional, resolutely tolerant of every type of thought. Yet it is important for us as theologians to try to bring together the whole human experience to which we have access into a unity, to see how it fits with the birth of our Lord Jesus Christ according to the flesh. Unless we do that, our concern for theology will succeed only in meriting the name that used to be given to Oxford theology, 'The final honours school of the archaeology of the christian religion'. When an attempt was being made at Cambridge to introduce a theological tripos in the 1850s, F. J. A. Hort, who was perhaps the greatest of the nineteenth-century Cambridge theologians, objected on the grounds that theology is a study which always becomes corrupted by being pursued exclusively. It is not good enough to make a pious nod towards the Greece and Rome of the Martyrology by studying the Eastern fathers or by reading the latest speeches of the Pope. Of course, no attempt to bring together all human experience in the light of the birth of the Christ-child could ever be altogether successful. But we cannot dispense ourselves from making the attempt. The task of writing a Christmas Martyrology is a task laid on us all, on each theological generation.

Christmas Day

The stories of the conception and birth of Jesus tell us not only about what happened when the Word was made flesh; they are concerned with what happens whenever the Word is being embodied in our world, at whatever time this may be. Time is so significant for us in our relationship with God. We meet him, and he comes to meet us, not on some timeless plane but at very definite times. The coming of the Word in our flesh was a coming into the time of our flesh; it was when the fullness of time (the appointed time) had come that God sent forth his Son, born of a woman. Gabriel says to Zechariah that his words will be fulfilled in their time, and the time comes for Elizabeth to be delivered. Then, while Joseph and Mary are at Bethlehem to be enrolled in the census of Caesar Augustus the days were fulfilled that Mary should be delivered. Later, Luke will tell us that the child was called Jesus when the eight days were full for circumcizing him. Luke will also speak of what happened when the days were fulfilled for Jesus to be taken up and when the days of Pentecost had fully come. The Word may be born of the Father before time began, but when he is born in time he gives time its due significance. Time preserves that significance when we turn to consider our own coming to birth from God. Like Mary we have to wait for the right time to be delivered of the Word. We have to wait for the right time to do what has to be done. And in this we are not dissimilar to the Son himself, for he waited to receive from his Father what he called his *hour*, the right time.

When we are concerned with doing God's will it matters, obviously, that we do the right thing; but it also matters that we do it at the right time. What might otherwise be a good action will be imprudent (and therefore lacking in goodness) if it is not done at the right time. Just as significantly, there may be actions which at some time of our lives we find we cannot do. We may be stuck fast in some habit and try as we will we cannot break free from it. This is by no means always a matter of bad will on our part; it may just as easily be that as yet the days are not fulfilled, our hour having not yet come. Until that time the question of guilt hardly arises: the situation is pre-moral. But when suddenly we find we can do it if we want to, moral considerations can properly be called into play. And how do we know when the time is right? No query about discernment can really be answered in the abstract, yet there do seem to be two elements very generally involved. First there is a subjective element, which turns on my self-knowledge. When are certain lines in my life starting to converge? When am I coming to a point when I will be able to make a move? But secondly, we are all public persons. We live in a world of clock-time, a shared world which has calendars and workdays and holidays. In the world of the Church we have feast days and fast days, Sundays and week-days, various seasons and ranks of celebration, solemnities and feasts and commemorations of saints. Even the natural world has its public time. The Book of Genesis suggests that God created the sun and the moon for the sake of the calendar, so that there could be a proper rhythm in our social lives. Days of shared significance in all these ways can help us to discover when it is time for us to move, to move on to a new stage in our service of God, to move into a new phase of our relationship with him, just as Mary did when the days were fulfilled and she brought forth her first-born son. Often enough we will find that the right time for us falls at some public time, some major anniversary or major feast. The subjective and the shared often coincide in our lives. Public occasions, we discover, give just the right weight to some private renewing. It happened like that with the Lord himself, as he waited for his hour from the Father. That hour was so personal between himself and the Father and yet, whichever year of his life it was to come it was bound to come at Passover and in Jerusalem. So perhaps we can let the rhythm of the liturgical year help us find ourselves. In all this the example of our Lady is there to aid us because, like the woman of the Apocalypse, sun-clothed, moon-shod, the Zodiac as diadem, Mary has time not as a threat to her integrity but as an adornment; and yet she belongs to time, sym-bolically being Virgo, just one of the twelve zodiacal signs. She ponders in her heart and thereby comes to know what her time is; and yet she does what she finds it in herself to do at a shared time, when the eighth day was fulfilled.

On one particular day Mary brings forth her son, her first-born, the one in whom all God's dealings with us and ours with him are focussed, the Word made flesh. Both word and flesh are equally significant here: neither is swallowed up by the other, and neither is lost in the other. The Word which God speaks to us in the human flesh of Jesus is not a different word from the word he speaks to us in the words of others. As Rupert of Deutz has it:

> Of old, God wrote a book by which in many words one Word has uttered. Today [at Christmas and in the whole Christian dispensation] he has opened a book for us in which by one Word many words are said. This is the book which has for its pages and for writing the word of the Father. The greatest of all books is the incarnate Son, because just as through writing words are joined to a page, so by assuming a human nature the Word of God is joined to flesh.[39]

Jesus is the *Verbum Dei abbreviatum*, the Word of God in shorthand, brought to small compass; but that does not make the written Word of God any less valid and significant. God concentrated the whole of the Scriptures, his word, in the womb of the Virgin; but the resonance of that Word in Scripture remains his word. Before Christ's flesh existed Zion the Blessed had brought forth the self-same Christ and Word that Mary brought forth when the days were fulfilled that she should be delivered. Without the words of Scripture the Word made flesh would scarcely have been recognizable. He would have made no sense, would not and could not have been significant, a sign, for us.

This remains the pattern of Christian worship. We are first put into the presence of the Scriptures, the presence of the Word as words. Like Mary who accepted her prophetic calling to bear the Word of God the Church first prophesies with her tongue. First of all, as we listen, she proclaims the Word of God to us in words. And only after this do we take and eat, take and drink. Only once we have listened does the Word come to flesh, to matter, to transform it into his own substantial presence. Without the Word of God as words, the shape of God's revelation is distorted. There is scripture reading in all the sacraments, and on all the occasions when the Church meets for worship. That is as real a communion with the Word of God as the subsequent sacramental communion with him. Indeed, without the prior communion in the Word as words, the communion in the sacrament runs the risk of becoming superstitious, a communing with a figment of our own imagination. Men make gods in their image; and even Christians are not immune from the temptation so to remake their Lord. Our images of Jesus are corrected by the witness of Scripture to him, whether in the gospels or in the rest of the New Testament and the Old – for the one God is the Author of both Testaments. All celebration requires this proclamation of the Word of God so that we, like Mary, can first conceive him in our hearts before we receive him into our hands and mouths.

None of this is easy for us because we lost a scriptural culture a very long time ago. In the liturgy we are normally presented with snippets of the Old and New Testaments, often so short that they make little sense on their own. It is assumed, frequently unwarrantably, that most of us have a context in which we can place the very brief extracts we hear read to us. But since they will not make sense until we do have such a context it is up to us to provide it. The call to renewal is an invitation to become soaked in the Word of God, to become people of one Book in a world that is full of books. Understanding of God's revelation will come only if we read and keep on reading the Bible, filling our minds and hearts with its words so that they became the atmosphere we live in. The longer passages of Scriptures read to us at the Office of Readings are a great help: they make the Bible seem less of a vast area of untrodden forest. Filling in the gaps by our own reading will help. The New Testament is read to us almost in its entirety at Mass, and over the years this too should sink deep into us. Even here, however, it would do no harm to look at the tiny passages which are not read publicly. But whatever way we choose the point of it all is clear enough: ignorance of the Scriptures is ignorance of Christ. Familiarizing ourselves with any part of the Scriptures is familiarizing ourselves with our Lord. It is becoming, like Mary, the matrix in which he was and is conceived, so that when the days are fulfilled he can be brought forth for the world's salvation.

Feast of the Holy Family[40]

For the Old Testament community, Jerusalem with its temple was the place chosen by God for his work of assembling his people into one. First of all, that referred to Israel herself, his chosen people, his first love. The tragic division between North and South after the reign of Solomon was seen most obviously in the setting up, over against Jerusalem, of alternative centres of national unity. As time went on, in the southern kingdom, all other places of sacrifice were rooted out, so that Jerusalem could better fulfil its task of uniting the nation. But secondly, the attractive force of Jerusalem has been universal. *Urbs Jerusalem beata, dicta 'Pacis Visio'*. The very name of Jerusalem is eloquent of a vision of peace and unity, of the assembling of the many tribes of the earth into a single people of God. At times that rang pretty hollow, but Jerusalem, even to our own day, has never lost that haunting power over people's hearts and minds as a city of all mankind, a city of peace, a city in which all peoples have citizen rights. Jesus himself acknowledged it when, at the age of twelve when he could begin to make decisions for himself, he endorsed his parents' attitudes to the city by going up with them to keep the feast of Passover in Jerusalem. He would have joined, no doubt, in the pilgrimage psalms, the 'psalms of ascent' as they are called, singing of how glad and happy he was when people first said to him, Let us go to the house of the Lord, of how his mouth had been filled with laughter and his tongue with singing. The joy of going up to Jerusalem was an anticipation of the great joy that there would be for all nations at the great ingathering to the marriage supper of the Lamb. Where else would Jesus be found except in the Jerusalem temple, this Jesus who was going to be lifted up to draw all things to himself, this Jesus who would gather into one the children of God who were scattered abroad over the face of the earth. Obviously, he belonged with Jerusalem.

This pilgrimage of the boy Jesus from his family home still has power to speak to us who are not Jews of the first century of the Common Era. This particular pilgrimage is a very Jewish thing: yet it is also a sort of sacrament of any and all human living. The Hebrew Bible finishes with the Books of Chronicles whose last words are 'Go up!'

> Thus says Cyrus, king of Persia: 'The Lord, the God of heaven, has given me all the kingdoms of the earth; and he has charged me to build him a house in Jerusalem, which is in Judah. Whoever there is among you of all his people, the Lord his God be with him. Let him go up.'[41]

Appeal has been made to these words at all the times of Jewish return to the Land which was promised to Abraham and his children for ever. It is the word on which Jesus acted when he followed the custom of his parents and also *went up* to Jerusalem.[42] It is a terribly Jewish affair, this pilgrimage; and yet it can image life itself, which is always some sort of departure in prospect of some kind of arrival. We leave everything, sometimes geographically, but always and certainly in one way or another. Peter tells Jesus that he and the other disciples have left everything and followed him. They have set out on his road. And in the story of the adolescent Jesus in Jerusalem we get our first hint of what that road will be. The disciples' following of Jesus means that they must make his destiny their own. That involves shaking off and leaving behind anything that might encumber a journey.

In the story of the losing and finding of the boy Jesus in the Temple the major obstacle to the journey of Jesus appears to be all that is meant by 'family'. Family gets Jesus to Jerusalem in the first place, but it also tries to recover him prematurely once he has arrived. The day will come when it will try to prevent him returning there when it really matters. The experience that the *familiar* gets in the way is common to very many Christians. House, brothers, sisters, father, mother, children, are part of what Peter and the others had to leave in order to follow Jesus. The pattern goes back to Abraham, who had to leave his father and his father's house, and it goes on to our own time. It is the pattern of the dark night of mysticism and of the dark night of political involvement. Families are not ultimates. Of course, there can be no excuse for not following the Christian ways of justice and love with our families: but still, they are not absolutes. Modern psychology concurs with this when it suggests that we have to break with our families if we are to find ourselves. A man has to be sure that he is not his father, even though he will not be at all mature until he can forgive his father for being as he is, and accept him. There is nothing absolute about a family, not a biological family nor those families which are our local and national institutions, nor even the religious communities which have adopted us and which we have chosen to make our families. Neither blood nor soil, neither nature nor nurture, can be allowed to have the last word in deciding who we are to be. We are not to allow any family to displace our direct and immediate relationship with God. The pilgrimage of Jesus led him to this discovery in the Jerusalem Temple when he was twelve years old. He found out that there was a higher claim on him than the claims of Mary and Joseph. For us, too, there is a sort of inbuilt principle of unpredictability in the Word of God that can divide our psyche from our true life. It can call us to something for which we are not programmed by our families, by all that is familiar to us. When it does call us, then we have to choose to save our lives or lose them, to remain settled or to involve ourselves with the destiny of Jesus of Nazareth, to join that pilgrimage to Jerusalem which was mapped out at his adolescence but trodden in deadly earnest in his manhood.

We have to distance ourselves from even the holiest of things for the sake of God, as Jesus distanced himself even from Mary and Joseph. We may not define ourselves in terms of even the highest of categories, the most godly of institutions. Home in all this is more a symbol than a place, more a state of mind than a building. Home is where we feel at home; and God seems to have difficulty in dealing with us until this power of the familiar is broken. It is there in the Holy Family. The first great break-up occurs when Jesus at twelve years old contrasts the One he calls his Father with the one Mary calls his father. Mary says to Jesus, 'Your father and I have sought you sorrowing;'[43] but Jesus says that he must be in his Father's house, concerned about his Father's affairs. This is a move which all Christians must make: 'Call no man your father on earth, for one is your Father, the heavenly One.'[44] In becoming Christians at all, we stand where Jesus stands, being born again from on high. And so, traditionally, the first word the newly baptized Christian says is 'Father', as he begins the Lord's Prayer, *the* Prayer, as patristic writers so often call it.

In the re-ordered Liturgy, the Lord's Prayer is solemnly recited three times a day, at Mass, Lauds and Vespers. At Office, in accordance with a venerable tradition, it has the place of honour at the end of the intercessions, a summing up of all that we ask God. The intention is obviously that the Our Father should be recited with all care and devotion at these points, not tacked on as a useless appendage, a popular prayer which everyone knows and no one attends to. The introduction to the Prayer at both Mass and Office is meant to prepare us for the seriousness of what we are about when we pray like this. Like the catechumens before baptism we are alerted and instructed: the Latin of the typical introduction says literally that we are alerted by saving precepts and instructed by divine commands. Almost all Christian liturgies have some such introduction to the Lord's Prayer, some way of reminding us what a weighty matter it is to come before the Father in the very words of Jesus, to stand where he stands. This prayer, in Tertullian's words, is 'a breviary (or condensation) of the entire gospel'.[45] When the great writers of Christian antiquity wanted to produce a work on prayer they normally and naturally wrote a commentary on this precise prayer. At the Mass, it functions like a prolonged Amen to the Eucharistic Prayer, succinctly recapping the major themes that the Eucharistic Prayer has spelled out at greater length. Like the Thanksgiving Prayer it is addressed to the Father; like it, too, it is a prayer of the whole Christian people. It prays God to hallow his name, to show that his name is holy; and the Eucharistic Prayer has dwelt at length on the holiness of God, joining with angels and archangels and all the warriors of heaven's army to sing the Trisagion, the Thrice-Holy Hymn, the never-ending hymn of God's glory. The Lord's Prayer also asks that God's kingdom may come. Alternatively, as in the primitive text of the Prayer in Luke's version, it asks that God's Holy Spirit may come upon us and cleanse us. The two are interchangeable for, as Paul says, the Kingdom is peace and joy in the Holy Spirit. In other words we have here, just as we have at Mass, a prayer of *epiclesis*, a calling down of the Holy Spirit to transform the kingdoms of this world into the Kingdom of God and of his Christ. We ask, as we ask when making Eucharist, that God will give us a pledge and foretaste of the new heaven and new earth, where his will may be done as it is in heaven. Then, as the Our Father unfolds, we find ourselves praying for our daily bread, the sign of the Bread of the Eucharist. And we ask God to forgive us, as we have asked for forgiveness in longer ways, and as we have been assured of forgiveness in the Lord's words about his Cup of the New Covenant, the chalice of his Blood, poured out so that sins may be forgiven. Finally, we ask to be delivered from evil, as we have asked for deliverance from final damnation in the Canon of the Mass.

And so when we pray the Our Father 'solemnly' three times during the day we might take those opportunities to recollect ourselves in the context of the great truths of the gospel, the truths which are effected in us at Baptism and in Communion. The hope is that day by day we shall recover something of the freshness of the time when (theoretically) we first said the Our Father, the moment of our Baptism. It is not an attempt to keep us infantile, to hold us in childish attitudes to God, to prevent us from growing up. Christians are not meant to be Peter Pans. The first words of our Lord are words that refer to God as his Father, but they are spoken in the moment of his growing up, of his breaking loose from the familiar as limiting so as to find it again in a new way. It is at the moment when Jesus calls God his Father that he ceases to be a child. 'Child,' says Mary, 'why have you thus dealt with us?'[46] But he was not a child any more. He was what Luke calls a 'boy': and that is the word that describes both Israel and David in the Benedictus, a servant, a full-grown man. The joy of the Our Father, like the joy of the boy Jesus in the Temple, is the joy of discovering the glorious liberty of the sons of God, of all those who, as the Liturgy of Baptism has it, call God their Father in the midst of the Church.

The Epiphany

When Jesus was born in Bethlehem of Judaea in the days of Herod the king, angels gospelled great joy to shepherds in the dark, to people who were despised and stigmatized. But the joy of the presence of God in our flesh was not confined to shepherds, and not even to all the people of God, to all Israel. When Jesus was born in Bethlehem of Judaea in the days of Herod the king, behold wise men from the East came to Jerusalem seeking him, and they too as they found him rejoiced with exceeding great joy. The coming of the wise men was a new mystery of joy, different in kind from that of the shepherds yet joy which, as with theirs, we are invited to enter. Jesus is 'a Saviour, which is Christ the Lord'.[47] He is a healer, then, a man who heals hearts and memories, who 'forgives all our guilt and heals every one of our ills',[48] as the psalmist says. But he is sought not only by people whose immediate need is healing and forgiveness, although everyone does need healing and forgiveness. He is sought by those whose needs are different from this, yet whose vocation to him is just as genuine as that of the shepherds. The shepherds have a direct and personal message pointing them to Jesus, that direct and personal message we call an Angel. The wise men, on the other hand, are drawn to him because of an inference from the movement of the stars, because of study, because of scientific observation. Wise men come to the Christ-child from the East: magi, a word from the same root as 'magician', not surprisingly in a world where anyone who could predict an aspect of the future seemed preternatural to people who found the world utterly unpredictable; star-gazers, astronomers and astrologers in one; perhaps priests of Zoroaster, priests of Persian fire-worship. At the start of Matthew's gospel, the most thoroughly Jewish of the Synoptic gospels, there come to Bethlehem these pagans from the utterly non-Jewish world in the East.

As Matthew understands it they come as first-fruits of the Gentile

61

world, an anticipation of the pagans who will come into view at the end of the gospel as Jesus tells his disciples to go out into all the world and preach the Good News to all creation. That is why the feast of the Epiphany is the traditional day of concentrated prayer for the missionary outreach of the Church. The final epiphany of Jesus will involve the whole world coming to him, bearing their gifts, as the gospel is preached to the ends of the earth. But how plausible is all this to us now? Can we fairly expect that the nations of the world will come in, bringing their gifts to this Jesus who is so Jewish and whom we have made so European? The probabilities are heavily weighted against it. Even traditionally Christian countries are no longer Christian in any meaningful way. The percentage of Christians in the world's population goes down rapidly from year to year. Many missionaries seem to have lost heart about simply preaching the gospel. They spend their time mainly in assisting the economic and social development of the countries where they work – a worthwhile and Christian thing to do, evidently, but not missionary work as traditionally understood. The world leaves Christianity on one side. Perhaps when we celebrate the feast of the Epiphany we should do so by taking a Passion-play view of the Church year, just recalling what it was like when the Lord Jesus first appeared and not looking to the story of the wise men to interpret some future coming of the Lord. Perhaps we would be best advised to give up waiting in joyful hope for any future epiphany on a world scale.

But no: we have our orders. Missionary concern and missionary action is not an optional concern for the Church or for any Christian. The mission of the Church in the strict sense of the term is directed to all those who have not yet heard the gospel, whether groups or individuals. In that basic sense of missionary, the Church, as the Second Vatican Council affirmed, is 'missionary by her very nature'.[49] When the Church attempts to preach the gospel to all creation she is acting on the innermost requirements of her own catholicity. A church which is not actively missionary is not actively catholic, that is, universal. And a church which is not actively missionary is a monster, because the Church is the embodiment of the mission of the Son and of the Holy Spirit from the Father. We share the nature of God, not simply in being able to stand before the Father as sons and daughters in the Son, filled with the Spirit that unites Father and Son, and therefore being people who face the Father. We also share his nature by going before his face: by

62

being sent on mission by the Father, as he sends his Son and his Holy Spirit. In case there should be any doubt, Jesus left clear instructions on the matter; and his Spirit, at the beginning of the Church's life, drove people out into the wider world to take the message to others. The Church's pilgrimage on earth takes the form of an envoy's journey. 'God's intention', says Clement of Alexandria, 'is the salvation of man, and this intention is called "Church".'[50] The more deeply we enter the mystery of the Church the more missionary our spirit should be. You see it in those two ecclesial men, Francis and Dominic: Francis traipsing off to the Moslem Court and Dominic constantly chafing with the desire to preach to the Cuman Tartars. The Council's decree on missions points to just some of the ways in which everyone in the Church can fulfil their responsibility for the preaching of the Good News, even those Christians who live an enclosed life in monasteries. They too 'by their prayers, works of penance and sufferings [one might have hoped there for a reference also to "joy"] play a part in the world's conversion'.[51]

The wise men from the East, then, should speak to us of the universality of the Church. They represent, we remember, the wisdom that is outside Israel, outside the religious and cultural tradition which gave birth to Jesus. Yet it is questions stemming from pagan wisdom that bring them to Jesus, the King of the Jews. They come to him with the baggage of various concerns, under the goad of various interests. We may see their gifts as much as indications of those interests as pointers to the role Jesus would play in their view of him. First of all they bring gold. Gold, the sweat of the sun, the metal that indicates politics and economics, the substance from which royal insignia are fashioned and in which trade is conducted. They bring frankincense, the material of worship, the stuff of the cult of God or the gods; and as wise men they would naturally ask questions of a theological sort, questions about the divine. Lastly, they bring myrrh, the ointment that reeks of death, itself the supreme question mark set against all the activities of man. The gospel of Matthew offers Jesus as an answer to all these questionings, whether political and social, or theological or ethical and philosophical. To the structure of the Gospel belong not only the simple faith of the shepherds that can take an angel's words on trust but also the deepest speculations of the human mind as it strives towards meaning and truth in pagan culture and pagan religion.

So the mission of the Church is not only the preaching of the gospel word. It includes as well the gathering up of possible pointers to the gospel. A missionary spirit means being ready and willing to see what there is in ways that are foreign to us which may lead people to Christ. Not being all-accepting in an uncritical fashion but certainly looking hard at the strange people we meet with their odd ways of thought for directions they could follow to arrive for themselves at the one Lord, who is our Lord, the King of the Jews. There is a quite unexpected passage in St Augustine's *Retractations* (a book he wrote at the end of his life to say where he had been mistaken in each of his previous books) where he thinks back over what he had once said about pagan religions and corrects himself. His last word on the subject is this:

> The reality itself, which is now called the Christian religion, was also present among the ancients and was not absent from the very beginning of the human race until Christ appeared in the flesh. Then from that point onwards the true religion, which had always existed, began to be called the Christian religion.[52]

There are some peculiar ways to Christ, but if they do lead to him then his light shines all the way down them. The magi set out in their journey as a result of what they learned through their own traditions. They saw a star rising, and their traditional wisdom taught them to interpret the event as a call to love. Through their own cultural media they sought a Messiah, and the seeking moved them in the right direction. But notice that, while their quest is the right quest, in the right direction, it does not come to its goal until the place where their questing can end is pointed out to them by other people. And this is the place of the missionary task. Jesus is *our* Lord; but he is our *Lord*. We cannot take him to another people as though he were ours to dispose of; but what we can do is to name the Name of Jesus on the quest of Everyman. We cannot short-circuit the long labour involved in another's journey as not really necessary because we happen to know in advance all about the journey's end. Rather, we need to enter sympathetically on the quests that other people embark on, and must embark on if they are to find Jesus. At the end of a road very different from that we first took ourselves we shall find the same Jesus, but showing himself to us in radically new fashions as the answer to quite new questions. This refreshment in our sense of revelation can happen whenever we experience the ways of worship of others, for example; the Catholic worship of the ancient Oriental churches or the new prayer styles that have evolved of late in our own society. If we are truly Catholic, we shall not confuse the Catholic gospel with the Roman rite, venerable and life-giving as it is. What matters is to love the Lord himself: to seek God and not to seek any particular way of worship.

St Paul says that a Christian is one who loves the epiphany of the Lord, his appearing and showing of himself to us. On the Epiphany the Church's Liturgy also celebrates how Jesus revealed his glory at the wedding feast at Cana; and we celebrate too the baptism of Jesus by John in the Jordan. But, as the White Queen said to Alice, it is a poor sort of memory that only works backwards. With the wise men and the wedding and the baptism we celebrate the supreme epiphany of the glory of our great God and of our Saviour Jesus Christ, that is, his appearing in glory at the end of time. Love for that appearing is meant to permeate our love for all the preliminary epiphanies; and we love them aright when our delight in them does not dilute our longing for the last and greatest epiphany. Whenever the Lord reveals himself amongst us we are to look forward all the more eagerly to what is still to be. We are given the eucharistic Bread and the bread of the Word as *Viaticum*, food for our pilgrimage, rations for the way. We are given the wine of the Eucharist and the wine of song and psalm to cheer our hearts in this our exile. But they are intended to make us more hungry and more thirsty for what we still have only in promise and fore-shadowing. Blessed, happy, fortunate are those who hunger and thirst like this, who still crave for God's great epiphany even though they have already been filled with good things. Happy are they, says the Lord himself, because they will have their fill.

Ash Wednesday

In the Liturgy of Ash Wednesday, we are presented with an extract from the Sermon on the Mount which is meant to serve as a programme for Christian living during the next forty days.

> Take heed that you perform not your righteousness before men, to be seen of them, else you have no reward with your Father who is in heaven. Therefore when thou doest alms, sound not a trumpet before thee, as the hypocrites do in the synagogues and in the streets, that they may have glory of men. Amen, I say to you, they have received their reward. But when thou doest alms, let not thy left hand know what thy right hand is doing, that thine alms may be in secret; and thy Father who sees in secret shall recompense thee. And when you pray, you shall not be as the hypocrites, for they love to stand and pray in the synagogues, and in the corners of the streets, that they may be seen of men. Amen, I say to you, they have received their reward. But thou, when thou prayest, enter into thine inner room, and having shut thy door, pray to thy Father who is in secret; and thy Father who sees in secret shall recompense thee . . . Moreover, when you fast, be not as the hypocrites, of a sad countenance, for they disfigure their faces, that they may be seen of men to fast. Amen, I say to you, they have received their reward. But thou, when thou fastest, anoint thy head and wash thy face, that thou be not seen of men to fast, but of thy Father who is in secret. And thy Father, who sees in secret, shall recompense thee.[53]

Lent is the time of the Church year when we try to get down to basics, the basics of God's love for us shown in the cross and resurrection of Jesus, and the basics of Christian living, the ways which express our acceptance of God's love for us. It is that latter acceptance, what we call 'faith', that justifies us, sets us right, makes us 'just right'. In the Catholic tradition, although we believe as much as any Lutheran that we are justified or set right by faith alone, faith for us does not refer simply to what goes on in our heads or in our hearts or both. Faith, if it is genuinely faith, is always embodied. Faith can be seen. 'I by my works will show you faith,'[54] as James says. Justice, the result of being set right in one's relationships by justification, is a visible thing. The fact that it can be seen in a false and distorted way, 'seen of men,' as Jesus puts it, does not mean that it should not be seen or embodied at all. Right relationship can and must be performed and expressed. In the Sermon on the Mount, following Jewish tradition, Jesus isolates three ways in which people do their justice, put their righteousness into expression: what we call the three eminent good works – of prayer, fasting and almsgiving. All three belong to the Christian celebration of Lent. But on Ash Wednesday, itself a day of fasting and abstinence, and the beginning of the great Lenten fast for those who adhere to an older tradition in the Church, it is appropriate, perhaps, to focus our attention on that whole business of fasting. What should be the place and significance of fasting for us?

The question is frequently sidestepped by thinking of the ways in which fasting may be useful for some purpose other than its primary one. Fasting might be valuable, for instance, as a means to the practice of almsgiving. We go without something, skipping a meal perhaps or giving up smoking for Lent, and we give what we have saved to some good cause. In recent years we have been encouraged to keep family fast days and to give the money we save to some international charity. Clearly, this is a good thing to do. And more than that, if we fasted in any of these ways and then proceeded to pocket the cash we had saved for our own self-indulgence in other ways, it is hard to see what virtue there would be in the fasting. Pope Leo the Great, whose sermons have marked so profoundly the Christian understanding of Lent, is quite firm on this point: 'Let our times of Christian fasting be fat and abound in the distribution of alms and in care for the poor; let everyone bestow on the weak and the destitute those dainties which he denies himself.'[55] Fasting without alms-giving, then, can be simply self-indulgence or else meanness towards oneself. Fasting with almsgiving, on the other hand, can make a difference, and a Christian difference at that, to the one world in which we live. One well dug in an Indian village, one fishing boat bought for a West Indian hamlet, can make the difference between life and death for a community. Yet this is to treat fasting as just a means to the practice of almsgiving, rather than as an eminent good work in its own right, that eminent good work it has been conceived to be throughout the tradition by Jews and Christians alike.

The same is true of fasting in hunger-strikes, a practice whose first Christian exponent appears to have been St Eusebius of Vercelli. In 355 he was locked up by the Arians to try to make him conform to their party, and he started to fast in protest, describing his motives to the priests and people of Italy by means of a circular letter. Mahatma Gandhi used the same method to try to win a change of heart from people in twentieth-century India. It would be possible to argue about the ethics of the practice but, once again, this kind of fasting is merely an instrumental thing. It does not get at the heart of the matter.

To clear the ground for a proper appreciation of fasting we need to mention and accept some of the provisos that Christian tradition has set around it. Fasting is of no Christian value unless it is integrated into a Christian life-style that includes relationship with God and with other people. The modern Roman Lectionary makes this point when, on the Thursday and Friday after Ash Wednesday, it has us read the fifty-eighth chapter of Isaiah, a plea for a fast or abstention from social evils and also, incidentally, the lection chosen by the Synagogue for the great fast of Yom Kippur, the Day of Atonement. Robert Herrick has a paraphrase of this text which is also a meditation upon it.

> Is this a fast, to keep the larder lean?
> And clean from fat of veals and sheep?
> Is it to quit the dish of flesh,
> Yet still to fill the platter high with fish?
> Is it to fast an hour, or ragg'd to go,
> Or show a down-cast look and sour:
> NO: 'tis a fast to dole thy sheaf of wheat and meat
> Unto the hungry soul.
> It is to fast from strife and old debate,
> And hate; to circumcise thy life.
> To show a heart grief-rent; to starve thy sin,
> Not bin; and that's to keep thy Lent.[56]

But notice that Isaiah 58 is addressed to people who are in fact fasting, just as the Church assumes on Ash Wednesday that we are

68

ourselves fasting when we hear the Sermon on the Mount read to us. To insist on the dangers that might accompany our fasting in such a way that the fasting itself is quietly ignored is to miss the point of the prophet's warnings. It could well be that in our polemics against false fasting we are as far from being relevant as that Danish pastor who made Kierkegaard so angry one Whit Sunday in the mid-nineteenth century, when he preached against monasticism, extinct in Denmark for three hundred years.

There is a second proviso which inevitably comes up when fasting is under review: the warning against Manicheism, against any disparagement of the goodness of God's creation. Some spiritual writers appear to be saying that fasting is a good thing because food and drink are bad things. They give the impression that if we are going to love God more, we must love what he has made less. St Thomas is quite clear that if people have that spirit in their fasting then it is without Christian value. Fasting for him is part of the virtue of temperance, which deals with right relationship to the concerns of the body. Temperance means doing our righteousness, acting just right, in the areas of food, drink and sexuality in particular. For Thomas there is only one vice in all this, the vice of insensibility, of not having a proper esteem for the goodness, delight and attractiveness of the world God has made for our good. Insensibility, or not being sensitive enough, is a vice not so much of the head as of the fingertips. It means that we are required to experience the world as good and delightful. We are morally obliged to take a proper pleasure from our senses, to be happily alive in our skins. Thomas would include here the touch of food and drink on our taste-buds, the touch of a perfume on our nostrils, and the specifically sensuous and genital pleasures of sex. Now clearly, he is not telling us that in order to be virtuous we must be libertines; but he is teaching that if we are not duly sensitive to the delights that creation gives to our skins, we are less virtuous than we ought to be. If I don't appreciate a malt whisky there is something wrong with me. If I am not moved by a woman's body I am lacking in goodness. And so fasting out of disdain for food, for all that business of cooking and eating and digesting and evacuating, is not an eminent good work. On the contrary, it is heresy in action. The desert fathers, those great heresy-hunters, used to set little tests for their visitors along these lines.

Jesus, nevertheless, assumes that his disciples will fast. He assumes it on the basis of Jewish tradition, just as that tradition assumed it from wider religious traditions. Fasting is a general religious custom. According to Thomas, indeed, it is part of the natural law: if we do not fast we somehow fail in our common humanity. On the opposite side of the golden mean from insensibility lies the temptation to grab and snatch at the world, to turn it into a source of our own satisfaction. The story of the Serpent tempting Adam and Eve in the Book of Genesis is our best image of this temptation. The world is there for man to use: all the trees of the garden are for Adam to enjoy. Yet there are limits built into the world's order: not everything is to be enjoyed by our consuming it. There is a right way to enjoy the tree in the midst of the garden; but that right way is not to eat its fruit. Thomas talks about a lion looking at a gazelle and seeing only meat, none of the beauty of its line and form, none of the grace of its movement. Adam oversteps the mark by trying to grab everything for himself. Perhaps the story speaks to men of the late twentieth century more powerfully than to any of their predecessors. For we know what it is to snatch at all the things of the earth so that our earth produces in response only thorns and thistles, or (even more horribly) nothing at all. Great lakes die when we treat the world as one huge apple to be demolished at a bite. Fasting is about training ourselves to distinguish our needs from our wants. When we fast or abstain we give ourselves a chance to discover what our real needs are. We learn not to sit up and beg every time we see something dangled in front of us which is good for food and a delight to the eyes and to be desired. John V. Taylor, in a highly germane book in this subject, *Enough is Enough*, gives examples of how our grabbing attitude thrusts evolution backwards, forcing calves and hens into a vegetable existence merely to ensure the sort of veal and the quantity of eggs we demand. Animals are to be used, rather, in accordance with the highest development of which they are capable. They are to be respected, as members of that great brotherhood and sisterhood which is nature, that vast friary of the cosmos of which Francis of Assisi is the supreme minstrel.

By the time that the first of the gospels was written, Christians were fasting regularly, perhaps even marking Friday in some such way. Mark explains why Christians fast in an image of marital presence and absence. The days will come when the Bridegroom will be taken away from them, and then they will fast, on that day. Fasting as a response to the presence and the absence of Christ the Bridegroom belongs in the new covenant of grace. It undergoes a change of meaning, however, in the waters of baptism. For Christians, the material and bodily world is the world which God has loved so much that he sent his Son to it. This story of how God turned to us, finally and definitively, in love and mercy, is good news, good tidings of great joy. It means that the world is for feasting. The story of the world is a *divina commedia*. And yet there is another, more sombre side to this picture. The world rejected the God who graciously accepted the world. At Easter, it is true, God signalled his refusal to accept our rejection. He keeps his offer open in the ever-open wounds of Jesus. But the world is still marked as the God-rejecting world. God's love was embodied in Jesus; and once-and-for-all that love, bodied forth in Jesus, was thrown out of our world. The man in whom the fulness of Godhead dwells bodily is not now available to us as part of the world around us. In order to attain his resurrection life we have to go out to him, pass over to him, die with him. To attain to him we have to die, sacramentally, mystically, morally and terminally. So we cannot simply affirm the world as it is now. We have to share in God's 'Yes' to the world: but that 'Yes' is always for us a 'Yes, but'. Our relation to the world is always nuanced. Fasting is the 'But', secondary to that 'Yes' we give to the world of things. God has said 'Yes' in glorifying the wounds of his Son, but they are still wounds nonetheless. Fasting from the food and drink of this present world is, for Christians, a sign of our expectation of the feasting in the new world, the world of the resurrection, on the food and drink of everlasting life. And just as you cannot pray without actually giving time to prayer, for it is nonsense to say that your life is a prayer if you never pray in a formal sense, so too you cannot learn to fast properly without some actual fasting from food. But the fasting is, ultimately, for the feasting. Abstaining throughout the forty days of Lent only makes sense if you are prepared, and preparing, to go alleluiatic throughout the fifty days of Easter.

Lent: the first Sunday[57]

'All occasions invite his mercies', wrote John Donne, 'and all times are his seasons.'[58] And yet some particular times are his particular seasons; and particular occasions can invite his particular mercies. His glory fills all heaven and earth, and yet his glory dwells in Jerusalem. He is from everlasting to everlasting, and yet he is born at a particular time and in a particular place. He is so born in order that Donne's affirmation may be realized, just as his glory dwelt in his temple high in Jerusalem so that we might see every wayside bush afire with God. The particular is for the sake of the universal, which means for the sake of every particular. One place, one city, one narrow strip of land is chosen so that the Law may go forth from Zion and the word of the Lord from Jerusalem, so that the earth may be full of the knowledge of the Lord as the waters cover the sea. One man is chosen so that in him all the nations of the earth may be blessed and may bless themselves, and so that in all those countries each one of us, every individual man and woman, may be blessed. And so when together we take stock of our lives before God, and when as individuals we reflect on our ways with God and his with us, we could do worse than to do this by considering his ways with those whom he has chosen in a particular way for the sake of all the particular individuals whom he has chosen. In principle, we could do this by reflecting on the life of absolutely any person, even of those persons who have never understood that God had any dealings with them and, indeed, that there was a God who might have to do with them. The reading of any biography or autobiography can give us, in principle, an insight into the ways of God, for we are all bound together in one bundle of life, and no man is an island.

But there are certain individuals whose lives have an altogether exceptional value in this kind of way. There are people of whom we would wish to say that while they are unique individuals, each with his own particular time in history and his particular place on the world's surface, they have nevertheless an exemplary value for all men everywhere. In the Judaeo-Christian tradition such individuals are above all the great people of Scripture. With their lives there coincided an acceptable time, a day of salvation, which can become living and actual again for us. In their lives and legends we find light for our living before God. The tradition to which we belong has produced great and complex philosophical systems, and this is right and proper. But Christianity is not a philosophy; it is a story, incarnate in particular people and as yet unfinished, although enough of the plot is written to indicate the nature of the ending. Christianity is a story which writes us. Abstract ideas may be the stuff of some religions, but the stuff of our faith is flesh and blood and bones, and sweat and sinews; our redemption is worked out by wood and iron and water, and by oil and bread and wine. And the first of these particular figures whom the Church evokes for us by story on the Lenten Sundays is Adam.

The first particular figure we meet in the story has such a universal significance that his name, Adam, itself means 'Man'. In the opening chapters of the story we have a hint of the whole subsequent development, as in the overture of an opera. But it is a very brief overture, and a very long time elapses before the Bible has anything of interest to say about Adam beyond the span of Genesis. When we reach St Paul, however, we find someone with a consuming interest in the figure of Adam. This interest was not in Adam for his own sake. It sprang from Paul's desire to speak about another particular historical individual born at about the same time as he himself, an individual whose significance was such that it affected every man. Paul found the language of Everyman in what Genesis told him about Adam, that Adam who from now on would be called 'the first Adam' and set over against Jesus of Nazareth as 'the second Adam'. It was only because of people's experience of Jesus that anyone wanted to say very much about Adam. And this, in turn, was because there were glaring omissions in the biblical portrait of Adam. Adam is man as he is, and man as man ought to be, but we are left with the haziest impression of the latter. We see what man is, what we would now call fallen man, but we see very little of man as he ought to be, of the potentialities of man. The universal sense that there is something amiss with our present condition, that man is not as he ought to be finds expression in the story of the first Adam. But just what is amiss, just what man ought to be, does not emerge at all clearly there. The Adam of the opening chapters of Genesis cannot really function in the way he was intended to function. But about two millenia ago certain people came to the conclusion that one man, whom some of them had known personally, was in all reality man as man was meant to be. They believed, and they told others that they believed, that in him they had for the first time seen real man. 'Behold the man!'[59] Behold Adam! And so the two pictures, of man as he is and of man as he ought to be, could now be drawn apart to some degree. The Adam of Genesis could stand for man as he is, and the second Adam, Jesus of Nazareth, for man as he ought to be. Yet both Adams must have something of the other about them. The first Adam must hint, at least, at how things might have been different. And if the second Adam is to be of any earthly use he must be shown to be a human being in the sense that we are, one of us. In the early centuries, the orthodox insisted, therefore, on the full humanity of Jesus. Whatever he did not share with us was not redeemed. But if you want to see man as he was made to be, then look beyond the hints in the story of the first Adam, that roughest of outlines, and you will see the full portrait in the second Adam, in Jesus of Nazareth as he is presented to us in the founding documents of the Church. He it is who successfully realized the human project in which the first Adam came to grief.

'Adam lay y-bounden, bounden in a wood.'[60] Adam, Everyman, lies tied up in a wood, outside the defined area of settlement, in a world that is not a human world. We know only too well this bounden side of our existence. For us as for Paul it is true to say that 'the good that I would, that I do not, and the evil that I would not, that I do'. We know also that the possibility of doing the evil that we would not lies not just within ourselves but in that wood in which we are y-bounden. We do not start life with unbounded possibilities of doing good and avoiding evil. The compounded errors of mankind have acquired a glacier-like momentum, almost like a force of nature. We know, as Cain was told, that sin lies crouching at the door, and that its desire is for us. In the myth of the temptation of Adam the serpent represents that incitement to sin that lies in the very structure of the world we inhabit. Every individual Adam, like the primordial Adam, finds sin already there. There is a tradition of evil, a standing invitation to betray ourselves and our vocation to be in the image of God. We start off, accordingly, disadvantaged. In the wood we find ourselves ousted from

74

the precincts of security, from the garden where we are at home. We find, too, that this invitation to evil has become internalized now. There is not only the world and the devil: there is also the flesh, human nature as it now is. We are porous, like those cryptic human figures in modern sculpture that are full of holes and gaps. Lent is our deliberate confrontation with all that. It begins by looking long and hard at those gaping apertures through which good drains out of our lives.

The temptation is to use all this as an excuse for opting out of responsibility, rather than as a cue for accepting it more profoundly. The serpent seduced me and I ate. What else could I have been expected to do? How can you possibly hold me responsible? But to be human at all means to be responsible, to be answerable. We hear 'the sound of the Lord God walking in the garden in the cool of the day'.[61] We hear his footsteps in nature and history. We find ourselves addressed: Where are you? And constantly we try to hide ourselves, refusing to be answerable, recoiling from the admission that we can be called quite fairly to account, not allowing that God has a right to ask us where we are. But the only way to redemption, to the second Adam, to what we are made to be and meant to be, is to answer the question, to become responsible, to let ourselves be judged. Only when Adam comes before God, naked and ashamed, can God's will to restore him be effective. Only when man is prepared to answer God's question, Where are you? can God reclothe his nakedness, as God clothed Adam with garments of skins to replace those absurd fig-leaves he plucked for himself, and as God intended to clothe him one day with the garments of light and incorruptibility, the resurrection body of Christ. 'Let me know myself: let me know you,' Augustine prayed.[62] Knowing ourselves is the first step on the road to conversion. Knowing where we are, and being prepared to admit God to that place which is where we are at in our lives, this is the quite indispensable first step on the journey towards recovery. The 'now' of the start of Lent will only be for us the acceptable time, the day of salvation, if we are prepared to stand before God as we really are and where we really are and admit that things are the way they are with us.

Lent: the second Sunday[63]

The description of man's condition in the opening chapters of Genesis is recognizable enough. Indeed, it is often only too easily recognizable. But as well as a description of the results of our sin these stories contain an analysis of what it is in which our sin consists. In each case it has something to do with man wanting not to be man but to be somehow divine. It is constituted by our failing to recognize the inbuilt limitations of being human. What could be, and what was meant to be, an horizon, comes to be thought of as a barrier, and even as the wall of a prison. We want to take a God's-eye-view of the world. When things go out of joint we tend to see every human situation in terms of a kind of masterful technology: we try to solve human relationships as we would a technological problem, standing outside the situation and manipulating it to get the best results. In the end this is to treat ourselves and others as objects, available materials for technical solutions. Yet there are many features of human life which will never be sorted out this side of the *Parousia* and which we throw even further out of joint when we try to resolve them. We build up for ourselves an ideal picture of what a community should be like, and then we set off in search of techniques whereby the blueprint may becomes the reality. We forget that we live in an imperfect and bounded world. We ignore the need to accept our limitations. This is not to say that anything goes, but that often enough we need to learn how to put up with situations, how to accept and how to forgive, and to go on and on accepting and forgiving, to recognize that we are flesh.

In the story of the Tower of Babel the same point is made, but with a slightly different emphasis.

As men migrated from the east, they found a plain in the land of Shinar and settled there. Then they said, Come, let us build ourselves a city and a tower with its top in the heavens, and let

76

us make a name for ourselves, lest we be scattered abroad upon the face of the whole earth.[64]

Here is the constant temptation to take short cuts; the refusal to get on with the business of living in the world before God; the premature insistence on living in the heavens, wanting to produce our own perfect society by our efforts while the world at large remains a world unfit for men to inhabit. Not that we should not eventually want a city with its top in the heavens, nor that we should not eventually want to be like gods. But there are various ways of wanting that. At the end of the Bible men do indeed live in such a city, but the city is the gift of God. Before the Flood God says that his Spirit will not abide in men for ever; but in and through Christ he freely gives us that Spirit in the age of the New Covenant. Men will indeed be as gods, as the fathers of the Church never cease to tell us. But we are to accept this deification as a gift from God, not to manufacture it from our own works. Unless you accept the kingdom of heaven as a little child, you will never enter it. The whole of the way God deals with man may be seen as a pedagogic method for teaching us how to accept a gift, the gift of a plan that will bring us more happiness than we could ever dream up for ourselves. And the first person God chooses so to teach us by is Abraham, whose call the Church reads to us among the Lections on the second Sunday of Lent.

Abraham, we say, is 'our father in faith',[65] the father of all believers, the man God chooses for the sake of all men, initiating in him the ways he wants to follow with all of us. Abraham is not only the first of believers; he is also their model, the man in whom the drama of faith is first sketched out. So in Abraham we can see ourselves. In our own life of faith we can recapitulate the story of the life of faith as lived out by him and his descendants. Biologists tell us that ontogenesis recapitulates phylogenesis; which means in English that the coming to be of the individual sums up the coming to be of the whole race. The human foetus in its mother's womb goes through all the stages of the long coming to be of humanity. At first it is like the amoeba, just managing to divide its cells. At one point it has gills like our fishy ancestors. At another point it has a tail, like our primate forbears. At some stage it has a coat of hair as in the days before man became the naked ape. This individual recapitulation of the biological evolution of the race has its parallel in the life of the spirit. Each one of us in our relationship

77

with God has to go through the stages of the relationship of the whole race with God. Abraham himself recapitulates the development of man with God until his own time.

> Terah took Abram his son and Lot his grandson, Abram's nephew, and Sarai his daughter-in-law, Abram's wife; and they went forth together from Ur of the Chaldeans to go into the land of Canaan; but when they came to Haran, they settled there . . . and Terah died in Haran.[66]

The aboriginal command to man to fill the earth, rejected mystically at Babel, was repeated to Terah, so the narrative suggests, in precise historical terms. Abram's father was told to leave Ur of the Chaldeans and go into the land of Canaan. But as the first men stopped at Babel and began to build a city so Terah and his family stopped at Haran: God's command found itself rejected in history. But then the command came to Abram: 'Go from your country and your kindred and your father's house to the land that I will show you.'[67]

The command to uproot oneself is repeated throughout the Scriptures. It is the command to Lazarus to uproot himself from death; the command to the people of God in the last conflict as the archetypal Babylon, Babel par excellence, is about to be destroyed, 'Come out of her, my people'.[68] Abraham was not rootless, he was uprooted. The difference is crucial. Having roots makes man human. Being brought up in a particular situation, loved by family and loving back, at home in a given place and a given culture, this is the very stuff of our humanity. It is hard for a person to make any kind of sense of the world if there was never a world where he belonged. But Abraham is told to leave these roots, to cease to define himself by a world already defined for him. For us to be healed and restored we have to abandon certain roots in society, culture and family. These have given us a world, but it is not yet the world of God. So Abraham went out, says the Letter to the Hebrews, 'not knowing where he was to go'.[69]

He went out in faith. He left Haran and thus avoided the temptation to conform completely to his world, to submit to the tyranny of the group. From being a city-dweller he entered the world of the Habiru (from which the name Hebrew will later come), those itinerant gypsy types who wandered for centuries up and down the Fertile Crescent. He became, in the technical term, *ger*, a stranger. Faith must always be earthed. Abraham our father was justified by faith, Paul tells us. But James, also speaking in the Spirit, says, Abraham our father was justified by works: faith was active along with his works, and faith was completed by works. Faith is visible: it takes on the form of a life-style. Only if you do such-and-such can you say that you have faith. For the rich young man whom Jesus met in the gospels had to be earthed by his selling everything he had and following the Christ: he could not bring himself to take so specific a course of action and so was without faith. Antony of Egypt heard the same call addressed to him during the Gospel one Sunday morning at the Divine Liturgy, and he, contrarywise, did what was demanded of him: he had faith. We too have heard the call to 'come forth'. We have been told to adopt a particular style of life, and have done so. But aside from this public profession of the Christian life there are also more private ways in which each of us will have to earth our faith from time to time. God will make demands on us, most typically perhaps through each other. If we refuse those demands our faith will stagnate and enter the rigor mortis. There are times when everything seems to come to a dead end in the Christian life. In our disenchantment we need, as a matter of life and death, the gift of discernment to enable us to know what to do next. The situation may be one of two sorts, and in each case it is lit up from within by the career of Abraham.

What Abraham really wanted was children and land to call his own. What God really wanted for Abraham was what Abraham really wanted for himself, as he always wants for us what we really want for ourselves. The end and the norm of a discipline is happiness, as St Thomas says. If we pierce through our superficial wants, through our surface ideas of what would constitute happiness for ourselves, and so touch our own deepest longings, we shall discover what it is that God wants for us. But supposing that what we want in this fundamental way is frustrated for years and years. What then shall we do?

The first thing that may be happening is that God knows that the time is not yet ripe for us to have what we really want. Probably, if we had it now we should only misuse it. On our part there will be a temptation to get something rather less than what we really want by an expedient. God said to Abraham, 'I will make your descendants as many as the dust of the earth.'[70] Yet as Abraham and his wife grew old they had not a single son. If God's promises were not, as it seemed, to materialize, very well, Abraham would have a son by some other woman in his own time. (In the Old

Testament situation this was not positively immoral.) But there was no divine blessing on the offspring of that union. God did not scorn the boy; he said that he would make a nation of the slave-woman's child as well. And yet no good came of it. 'He was a wild ass of a man, his hand against every man and every man's hand against his; and he dwelt over against all his kinsmen.'[71] Ishmael was not what God really wanted, just as he was not what Abraham really wanted, a son by Sarah. At certain times in our lives we, like Abraham, want something to show for ourselves, some stake in the future by which we will be remembered. And so we force ourselves into activity. We cannot manage to live in faith any longer; we are stagnating; we must produce; as individuals and as communities we cannot wait. In such cases what we bring forth does not carry the fullness of God's blessing. Moreover, it may mean that when God at last is really going to give us what we want we can no longer believe that it is happening. We have lost hope, as Abraham and Sarah lost all hope of the future save Ishmael, and so could not believe the message of the angels at Mamre. Doing just anything at all destroys the possibility of faith.

Alternatively, we may find ourselves in stagnation of a very different sort, where faith, if it is to survive, must be expressed not in waiting but in acting. God said to Abraham: 'Take your son, your only son Isaac whom you love, and go to the land of Moriah and offer him there as a burnt offering'.[72] God may demand some particular action from us, and until we do what he wants we are stymied. If we are stuck in the life of faith, say, in our prayer life it may be because we know deep down that there is something he wants from us – the abandonment of some deep-seated bad habit, perhaps, or a breakthrough in our relationship with another person, or forgiveness of a wrong done to us in the past. Unless we can give him what he wants, our faith dies. What he wants may even be the gift of something good and godly, our Isaac, our 'laughter', the joy of our heart, a gift and a blessing from God himself. When God asks this particular sacrifice of our father in faith it is not the burnt flesh of Isaac he wants but the heart of Abraham. He wants Abraham to have himself as his shield and his exceeding great reward. He wants to give Abraham himself and not his gifts. And so he tests him, in the hope that he will acknowledge Isaac as God's gift, not Abraham's work. Any couple is asked not to keep their child for themselves, not to make him their consolation. We too may be asked to detach ourselves from some cherished offspring, some good piece of work we have done, some reality we have built up from scratch. To live by faith is to be prepared to give up even the gifts of God. God may not in the end insist that we do actually lose our brainchild, as he did not insist on the sacrifice of Isaac. And yet he may make that ultimate demand, as he did of Mary when she stood by the cross and received another son in place of her firstborn. Can we say that God was unfair to Mary, when her firstborn was his Only-begotten Son?

In the last resort, living in faith means living in faith in the resurrection, in the light and strength of God's promise to make a new heaven and a new earth. When Abraham had made the sacrifice in his heart, he received back Isaac as though from the dead, never more to lose him. When Mary had made the sacrifice not only in her heart but had actually seen her hopes killed, she received back her Son not 'as though' from the dead but literally from the realm of death, never more to lose him. And that risen body of Jesus which had passed through physical destruction and the death of Mary's heart was indeed 'Isaac', laughter, the joy that no man could take from her.

Lent: the third Sunday[73]

There are three great Lenten readings from St John's gospel, and
all three are readings about Jesus meeting people, the Woman of
Samaria, the Man born Blind, and Lazarus. These stories aim to
put us in the picture about how Jesus once dealt with people, he
who is the same today as he was then, so that we in our turn can
put oursevles in the picture albeit in another way. Take the story
of Jesus and the Woman of Samaria. The woman belongs to a racial
group that few of us know anything about. Few people would
recognize a Samaritan woman if we saw one in the street. She
belongs to a very different kind of society from ours. And yet in the
way this story is told there is something about her with which all
of us can identify. There is something about this meeting with Jesus
which happens somewhere along the line in the meeting of every
man and woman with Jesus in the encounter that lasts a lifetime.

It begins with Jesus asking something from us. He says to the
woman, 'Give me a drink'.[74] On Good Friday John tells us that
Jesus said, 'I thirst', and that he said this 'in order to fulfil the
scripture perfectly'.[75] There is no single text which Jesus is quoting
or alluding to here, but the thirst of Christ is rooted deep, apparently, in the Scriptures, in the story of God's dealing with us from
the beginning. It is the whole of the Old Testament that Jesus is
bringing to its fulfilment here. Jesus focuses and manifests for us,
as clearly and as finally as can be, what the Father is like. In Jesus
thirsty we are shown God thirsty. In Jesus thirsty on the cross at
about the sixth hour, and in Jesus sitting by the side of the well at
about the sixth hour, worn out with his journey, we see God's basic
attitude towards us. He longs for something. He thirsts for something. He is related to the world not just as a creator and not just
as a lawgiver. He is related to the world as one who in some
extraordinary sense needs the world and longs for something from
it. There is no obvious sense in which God can need anything, not

even the whole of his creation. And yet still in some way he does long and thirst for it. That love-longing of God for us comes at the beginning of the story of his dealing with men. Salvation is about God longing for us and being racked with thirst for us. God wanting us so much more than we can ever want him.

But so often we treat the way to God as an obstacle course set up by God. Even the greatest gifts of his love can be made to seem like difficult obstacles which we have to circumvent, almost as though God has set up a maze between him and us so that we have to make every move right and every turn correct if we are going to reach him as our journey's end. People treat confession like that sometimes. They take infinite pains to say things in exactly the right way, and with some idea at the back of their minds that if they don't get it just right then confession won't work and absolution won't take and God won't really have forgiven them. Such people treat confession as a device God has grudgingly provided for us to use when we break our friendship with him. So grudging is the provision that we must take all care to comply with every last condition laid down. But no sacrament is the result of a grudging concession on the part of God. The sacrament is there because of God's thirst for us, his longing for us. When Jesus by his thirst has let us through to the thirst of God for us, and when the soldiers at the Passion, by offering him their sponge of sour wine, have let us see how people respond to that, then all that Jesus can say is 'Everything has been fulfilled.'[76] The heart of the matter has been laid bare. All that remains is for Jesus to bow his head and die. But on the other side of death, the first words he says to his apostles are words of forgiveness, words which commission the apostles to extend that forgiveness to others. Part of the weight of those first words of the risen Jesus to the apostles, as St John gives them, is the continuing thirst of the risen Jesus in the sacrament of forgiveness. Jesus, still thirsting with the thirst of God, could not wait to tell his apostles about forgiveness. That is always what comes first in the meeting between man or woman and God in Christ. The thirst of Jesus was a thirst that the Samaritan woman could not satisfy by water from Jacob's well but only by giving him her heart, her love, her faith. He was thirsting for her faith, as we say in the Preface at Mass today.

Mother Julian of Norwich saw this so clearly.

I saw in Christ a double thirst: one bodily, another ghostly [spiritual] . . . The same desire and thirst that he had upon the cross (which desire, longing and thirst, as to my sight, was in him from without beginning) the same hath he yet, and shall have unto the time that the last soul that shall be saved is come up to his bliss. For as verily as there is a property in God of ruth and pity, so verily there is a property in God of thirst and longing. And this property of longing and thirst cometh of the endless goodness of God, right as the property of pity cometh of his endless goodness. And though longing and pity are two sundry properties, in this standeth the point of the ghostly thirst: which is lasting in him as long as we be in need, drawing us up to his bliss . . . The longing and the ghostly thirst of Christ . . . lasteth and shall last till Doomsday.[77]

First comes this thirst and longing of the Lord for us. And, St John goes on: 'There was set there a vessel full of sour wine; so they put a sponge full of the sour wine on a stick and brought it to his mouth.'[78] Jesus accepts what is offered. At least as St John understands this incident there is nothing but compassion being shown. The soldiers, we are to presume, brought the wine for their own use; it was a popular drink in the hot climate, refreshing and thirst-quenching. What the soldiers had they were prepared to share. Jesus, on the judgement-seat of the cross, could have said to them, 'I was thirsty and you gave me to drink.'[79] He is no hero or ascetic, rejecting his basic bodily needs. He takes the help he is offered. He thirsts for more than sour wine. But refreshment in that heat is included in his total thirst. Taking what is offered is one step in taking all that the soldiers could offer.

He starts from where he is, from where others see him. In the case of the Samaritan woman he meets her as one with needs, but she meets him as a person with needs herself. In her we see ourselves. It is not necessary to start out with particular profound or super-refined needs in order to make contact with Jesus. He merely happens to be there when a person is seeking to fulfil and satisfy the needs of the moment, however trivial or however deep they may be. The Samaritan woman in need of water goes to the well like going to the shop to get an ounce of tobacco, and there he is. Yet from the point of view of Jesus this is not in fact casual or chance. He has been sitting there waiting for her. It has been a long journey. He has come all the way from the heart of God. After thirty years he is tired. He sits down. It is noon, the hour when he has to be

84

still, the hour when he is nailed to the cross with nothing to do but wait. He tells her he is thirsty. On the cross he will shout it aloud to anyone who will hear. And so, while a casual meeting from her point of view, it is planned from all eternity from his. Becoming a Christian is always like that. From our point of view it just happens; from God's it is predestined. Our need brings us somewhere, any- where, to where the need can be met. My need may be for food or drink or a smoke, or for a man or a woman. But when we arrive at where it is, there Jesus is sitting and waiting, with nothing to do but to wait for us. Of course even so it might have remained casual. But it did not. Jesus and the woman started to talk. The conver- sation turned to what he and she really wanted. Bit by bit it shifted from the ordinary want she had for water for her household to a more all-embracing need for water. It shifted to a need that covered all other needs, a longing that she could hardly put a name to. How she wanted things! It was because she wanted things so much that she finally found everything she could possibly want. It was because her wants were so strong and so fierce that she found everything she could ever have wanted, and so much more. Coming to Jesus will not work if you have little desire. It will work if you have some emotion and passion, some fire in your guts. 'Does he really seek God?'[80] is the basic question, according to the *Rule of St Benedict*.

The story of the Samaritan woman was and is meant to be read to people preparing for baptism. It is read during Lent, and Lent is for us who are already baptized a time of preparation for our official re-birthday on Easter Night. Easter is the official anniversary of our baptism, the Night when God raised Jesus from the dead and left the grave wide open. In Lent we try to remember how exciting it can be to be a Christian. We try to get back to what it was like at first, before we became elderly about it. The story of the Woman of Samaria is there to stir up in us something of that passionate wanting that is expected from people preparing for baptism. In the ancient Church such catechumens were given this psalm to sing: 'As a deer goes crazy looking for water in the desert so I am going crazy looking for you, my God'.[81] This they sang as they went to the well, the font, where Jesus was awaiting them. The story of the thirst of the Samaritan woman is meant to make us want things more, to want with a depth and an intensity like that of the thirsty man when the dehydrated tissues of his body cry out to be slaked. This woman who stands for us finds God on the basis of wanting fiercely whatever it is that she does want, and then discovering that

85

the homing point of all her fierce desire is Jesus. 'What do you have to do to become a saint?' St Thomas was asked. He replied in a word: '*Velle*, want it!'[82] As Julian says, 'Of the virtue of this longing in Christ we have to long again to him: without which no soul cometh to heaven.[83].

Lent: the fourth Sunday[84]

On the fourth Sunday of Lent the Church places before us the figure of David, the Lord's anointed, juxtaposed with that supremely Spirit-filled Man, whose death and resurrection we are preparing to celebrate, her own Lord Jesus Christ. The way of the Liturgy is also the way of the Bible, for Scripture discloses to us the true structure of our being by showing us someone else. As Robert Frost remarks, 'Society can never think things out'.[85] It has to see them acted out by actors, devoted actors at a sacrifice. The Bible shows us people who had to find their own vocation within the vocation of the whole people, and so let the story of Israel write the story of their lives. All true originality in any field comes not to destroy but to fulfil the central tradition. It issues from belonging as explicitly as possible to that tradition and from being able because of that belonging, to carry tradition forward. We trust original people only if we see that they have their roots firmly in the soil of the tradition of their art or craft. We trust the Picasso of all periods because we have seen in the Picasso of the early period superb examples of painting intelligible from the artists who went before him. We find the same pattern even with the Word of God made flesh, when we see Jesus as a pupil, sitting at the feet of the teachers in the Temple, before he became a rebel in Israel and even in some ways a rebel against Israel. And we see it in David, whose son Jesus was and who in his own life recapitulated the story of Israel and took that story forward. David lived out the vocation of Abraham, being called to leave his father and his father's house. He also lived out the vocation of Moses, being called from looking after sheep to shepherd Israel, to complete the still uncompleted Mosaic task of leading Israel into the promised Land.

There was, for example, a small and unimportant Canaanite town on the borders of the northern and southern tribes which neither tribal group had yet conquered, perhaps because it hardly seemed worth capturing. That small and unimportant town fell to David and he made it his capital and, more than that, the city which would be one day closest to the heart of three great world religions, a city whose vocation it was and is to be the City of Peace. David was above all the man of unity, the man who united Israel, and the man to whose reign Israel ever looked back as the time when the people of God was one and undivided. David created for a few years that unity which was the purpose of God for Israel, while her unity was itself meant to be the model and the growing point for the unity of all mankind. That Davidic vocation remains ours as members of Christ's Church. As the Second Vatican Council put it: 'The Church is a kind of sacrament or sign of intimate union with God and of the unity of all mankind; she is also the instrument for the achievement of such union and unity.'[86] From this angle, indeed, the Church can be experienced, at least in germ, wherever and whenever we see a sign of unity between men which also functions as a means for furthering the unity of mankind. Even at the level of two people that vocation is worthwhile. Think of how important the number two is in the New Testament, a reflection of the two strands of Israel–Judah which David gave his life's work to uniting. In Matthew's gospel it is again and again two people who come to Jesus to be healed and reconciled with their society, two men possessed by devils, two of the great multitude of the blind. Jesus sends out his disciples two by two to prepare the way before him for, as St Gregory the Great puts it, with less than two there could be no charity, no sign of the Kingdom of God. It is to two people, husband and wife perhaps, that the risen Jesus reveals himself in the Breaking of Bread on Emmaus Road. Their eyes were opened as were the eyes of Adam and Eve but this time, to follow Gregory the Great once more, in order to see the deification of their nature rather than their shame. The new and greater David, David's Son and David's Lord, Jesus of Nazareth, says that where two or three are gathered together in his name there he is in the midst of them. In any reconciliation of even two people, wherever two people become one spirit or one flesh, the Lord is at work and personally present, always there as the third.

From this point of view 'church' is a verb rather than a noun. 'Church' refers to the work of reconciliation between men. This suggests how our religious communities within the Church are meant to function. They have a never-ending task of becoming truly one, of reducing multiplicity to a unity which stifles no one but opens up to us a share in the unity of the Father and the Son, what we call the Holy Spirit. St Augustine, whose Rule Dominicans follow and who stands at the head of the canonical way of life, explains that he and his monastic brethren are called 'monks' because in their diversity they have become *one* in heart and mind, through the ardour of their love for the Christ who stands in the midst of them. We must never allow ourselves to settle for anything less than this monasticism, this becoming one, no matter how formidable the obstacles in its way. But whatever our particular vocation in the Church we must never belittle the Davidic task, the work of reconciliation within any group, large or small. As the rabbis put it:

He who brings discord to his house, it is as though he had brought discord to all Israel;
he who makes peace in his house, it is as though he had made peace in all Israel.[87]

Every Christian life is directed to some form of oneness, communion, *sobornost* as the Russians call it, with other men.

Not that it finishes there. By our baptism we are committed to being instruments, in one way or another, in the unifying of all mankind. Our local churches are gathered around the figure we call the bishop; and a bishop is precisely a sign and instrument of unity. All the extraordinarily enthusiastic things that Ignatius of Antioch has to say about bishops and their place in the Church are rooted in a sense of the bishop as a man of unity. Through his instrumentality in securing the concord and symphonic love of the Christian community, Jesus Christ is sung. And in the Church at large the Bishop of Rome has supremely the function of being a creative centre of unity, the expression of the mutual love of all the members of the body of Christ. You remember the ancient anagram: ROMA – AMOR. Rome is about love; and if it is not about love it is nothing. But all of us, and not just the Roman pope, have a duty to fulfil the function of Rome and Jerusalem as well as we can in our local situation, never reconciling ourselves to the disunity of Christianity or to the disunity of the family of man, but always keeping our eyes open to ways in which we can further that unity which is God's will and plan for the world.

The City of David has always haunted the Christian conscience. Where else other than Jerusalem could the Messiah suffer in order

89

to make men one? Where else could the Holy Spirit be poured out except upon the citadel of David, so that the word of the Lord might go forth from Jerusalem and the law of God from Zion? That Spirit, we say, is the go-between God, the love between men as he is the love between the Father and the Son. Not surprisingly, therefore, the primitive church in Jerusalem had a very strong sense of the practical implications of his outpouring. They focussed and expressed their awareness of unity in a voluntary communism, practising community of goods. Depending on one another for their material wellbeing seemed to follow from their common dependence on the risen Jesus whose Spirit was poured upon them. The Jerusalem church, no doubt idealized in the accounts we possess in the Book of the Acts, has continued to exercise a powerful attraction. Even in the failure of its experiment in community living, it, being dead, still speaks. Just as the Jerusalem-ideal of David failed after the reign of his son Solomon and yet gave birth in its dying to the deathless messianic hope of the people of God, so the Jerusalem church has lived on in the inspiration it offers men for a life based on more than their inherited or acquired expectations of the world. In Augustine's time, in the early days of many religious orders, in the Christian commune movements of this century and of the last few years, the Christianity of the City of David has permitted and enabled people to live in a different style from what they and others have made of the world up to now. In this way, despite its failure, it can be seen as the product of the genetic code of the twice-born, the life from water and the Holy Spirit that makes all things new. If we can manage to give this vision flesh and blood in our renewal of ourselves in Lent we shall be heirs of David and of David's Son. But in that attempt to live with one mind and one heart in God, with all its practical implications in mutual care and concern we may well fail, as we all know. Failure is, however, the customary Christian pattern: the pattern of Jesus, of the Eucharist, of the church in David's Jerusalem, of the great Christians of our own day. No matter. Just as at the end of Lent, beyond the death in failure of the Lord lies Easter, so beyond our deaths and the deaths of our Christian schemes lies the Jerusalem that is the gift of God, the city of peace, the centre that radiates unity.

Lent: the fifth Sunday[88]

Of the so-called 'writing prophets', those who have biblical books named after them, all but three were prophesying in the time when the fortunes of Israel and Judah were at their lowest, when disaster either threatened or had already occurred. Yet all these prophets found that the last word they had to say about God's dealings with Israel was a word not of disaster but of hope. (The last verse of Isaiah in our Bibles is a verse of threatening, but when read out in synagogue or printed in Hebrew Bibles the penultimate verse is repeated after it, so well do the Jews understand the God with whom they deal.) God promises his people a future and a hope. This hope is created by the promise of a new covenant which will include the former covenants but go an immeasurable distance beyond them. The prophets were very nearly at a loss for words when it came to describing the content or even the form of this hope. For some, it was a new exodus through the desert, with marvels outstripping those of the first exodus from Egypt. For others it was a return to the paradise of Eden, with the world's fierce beasts trained and a little child leading them all. For Ezekiel, it was going to be like resurrection from the dead, the restoration to life of the dry bones of the people of Israel. But in the years after the Exile, when the Jews were back in their own land, these promises could easily appear quite empty. True, they were back: but the reality of their situation fell impossibly short of a new garden of Eden. As years and centuries went by the quality of life deteriorated. Israel fell under the domination of one foreign power after another. The glory which had departed from the Temple, in Ezekiel's vision before the destruction of the 'joy of all the earth',[89] did not return in the time of Israel's restoration. Some folk reacted by a natural concentration on getting by and getting on in the world, reconciling themselves to the reality of the new situation and making the best of a bad job. Everyone agreed that the voice of prophecy had fallen

91

silent in Israel. But some individuals refused to yield to the general cynicism. They continued to accept the inspiration of the prophets, but they transferred their hopes of an historical future to a great and decisive act of God which would not so much be in time as be that which brought time to an end. There would be a Day of the Lord, with God as king. The desert would rejoice and blossom like the rose. There would even be a resurrection of the dead. But the day of all this was hidden, so they thought, in the secret plan of God. The task of those who stayed faithful to the conviction that the prophets had spoken under the inspiration of the Spirit of God was to wait quietly for that day, the day on which the dead would rise again. 'I know that my brother will rise again,' said Martha to Jesus as they stood by Lazarus' tomb; 'I know that he will rise again in the resurrection at the last day.' And in this gospel for the last Sunday of Lent Jesus answers her: 'I am the Resurrection.'[90]

'I *am* the Resurrection.' So often we think of resurrection as an affair of the past or of the distant future. We think about what happened to Jesus on the first Easter night, on that past date which we commemorate year by year and Sunday by Sunday. Or we think about resurrection in the future, casting our mind's eye on the world's end, when the present order of things comes to its close, the resurrection of the dead, the life of the age to come. We look back with gratitude and with wonder to that first Easter night; we wait with joyful hope for the coming of our Saviour Jesus Christ, for that last day when our brethren and we ourselves will rise again. Yet Jesus says to Mary not that he shall be, but that he *is*, Resurrection and Life. What are we to make of these words? For Martha they were merely a piece of information, true or false; for Lazarus they were a matter, literally, of life and death. If we are to be able to give them a cash value in our own lives we have to find ourselves somehow in the tomb with Lazarus, rather than in the sunlight outside the tomb with Martha. Only if we are in some way raised from death ourselves can we proclaim that Jesus is the Resurrection.

What does it mean to be dead? Death traps, it separates and it destroys. Lazarus was bound, a prisoner of his past, fixed forever in what he had done and had done to him. Lazarus was cut off from his family and friends, isolated in his loneliness. Lazarus was no longer a full human being but falling apart, disintegrating, smelling to high heaven. Am I in any way with Lazarus in all this, in some way already down amongst the dead men? If I am not, I will hardly be able to say that Jesus is already the Resurrection. If I am not dead now, then I cannot rise now.

This is one way of talking about Lenten self-examination. We examine our conscience by asking ourselves in what ways we are dead, in what ways we are falling apart, in what ways we are prisoners of our past. Certain habits, certain ways of thinking, certain attitudes may have us fast in their grip. Perhaps other people have played a particular game on us for so long that we cannot now stop playing it ourselves. Perhaps we think of ourselves in the way we have been conditioned to by others. Or it may be that we are dead from the neck up: getting our ideas from the same old newspaper and the same old spiritual books, year after year after year. Or, alternatively, dead from the waist down: no longer with any feelings worthy of the name, so that we cannot even imagine what it would be like to fall in love with someone again. Or perhaps we are caught in some vicious circle of being hurt and hurting back. Perhaps we cannot envisage any real change in the direction of our life. *In circuiti impii ambulant*: 'the wicked walk in a circle',[91] as the Psalmist says. But if this is the case, then we are in some way like Lazarus and so we enjoy, in some way, the hope of Resurrection now. The God in whom Christians believe does not keep life going on and on. He is, rather, the God who raises people from the dead.

What, then, may we expect that this God of ours will do? First, we must note that he will get to work in his own good time. The right time, the time God determines is, as often as not, the time when we are dead in such a way that we cannot raise ourselves. Jesus goes to wake Lazarus on the fourth day, and in Jewish tradition, a person does not really and properly die until three days after his apparent death. A man who is dead cannot rush things, nor use violence on himself. He can only wait and listen, to learn when the right time has come, and to trust that when that right time comes he will hear the voice of the Son of Man and be raised. Suppose that we have died, that our world has collapsed and that everything has fallen apart for us. Maybe it is through the shock of a bereavement. In such a situation we will rise when the time comes, but we must not rush things. We must respect the inherent rhythms of our emotional life, as God respects them.

Secondly, our faith in this God who raises the dead must involve real, not just notional, assent. We must really believe that the Spirit of God will give life to us, not on the last day but today, the today of the right time. Jesus, we are told, was angry because Lazarus was dead. Not that he blamed Lazarus for being dead, any more than he will necessarily blame us for whatever death we are in. But Lazarus, like us, was made for life, not for death. The Christian people believes in life, life more abounding, life for the body and for the spirit of man. So we have to be ready, when God's good time comes, to come out from our dead past, even with our grave-clothes still binding us tight. In all this perhaps the hardest thing is to let other people help set us loose. Lazarus emerges from the tomb at the voice of the Word of God, but he needs other people to loosen his shroud and help him start life again. Even when the time has come when we can forgive or forget, when we can start to fall in love again, when we are ready once more, like Lazarus, for festivity, we shall still need people to unbind us and set us free. We must allow others to absolve us, as the synonym from the Latin says. In the life of the Church that may happen in a variety of ways. Sometimes it will be a friend who unties us, perhaps one of our community. Sometimes it will be our next-door neighbour, perhaps someone in our parish. And sometimes it will be the person who stands officially for us and for all our fellow-Christians, for the Church at large and for the bishop, the centre of communion of the Church at large. Sometimes, that is to say, we can celebrate that absolving sacramentally with the priest, the representative of the people of God.

Jesus said to the people who were standing around to mourn Lazarus, 'Absolve him and let him go free.'[92] When other people do unbind us we shall know what it means to say that Jesus is the Resurrection. It will be a matter of life and death for us, or, better, of death and life. It will be a case of resurrection from the dead, the dead past of what we have made of our lives until now.

Palm Sunday: the entry into Jerusalem

It is part of the irony of the New Testament that when Jesus of Nazareth made his solemn entry into the holy city of Jerusalem just before his Passion, he did so in a situation heavy with the sense of imminent peril. For the same New Testament sees this same Jesus, in the light of his life, death and resurrection, as crucially engaged in any and every entry of human beings into the presence of the holy. 'I am the Door',[93] says the Jesus of John's gospel in one of those titles given to Jesus which were an early way of doing Christology, a primitive way of answering the question Jesus poses to everyone who comes into contact with him: 'Who do you say that I am?'[94] Christian tradition echoes this perception:

> He is the Door of the Father, the door through which Abraham goes in and Isaac and Jacob and the prophets and the apostles and the Church, the door through which they all make their way into the unity of God.[95]

Such titles as these are not honorific: they mean what they say. Think of a modern title like 'linkman' which says so precisely what a man's function is. It tells you what he is supposed to do, and what in fact he does do. 'The Door' is a description of what Jesus means for people, of the function he exercises in their regard. The office and function of a door is to enable people to come in and to go out. Like Janus, the pagan guardian of the door, and like his month January, the door looks both ways, permitting entrance and exit alike. The door is the condition of freedom. The city gate is what guards people, yet if the door of the city or the house is always locked, some men will die of starvation or suffocation. The doors of plague houses were nailed up so that they could only be barriers and not a passage, not a way in and out. Jesus as the Door is our means of access to holiness, and to happiness. On Palm Sunday he who is in his own person the gateway to God entered through the city gates of the holy city as its King. But he did so in all the ambiguity of his approaching Passion, in peril and under threat. On Good Friday he will be put outside the gates, deported to Mount Calvary which was 'without a city wall'. Contrariwise, in the new Jerusalem the gates of the city lie ever open. 'Behold', says the Christ of the Apocalypse, 'I have set before you an open door, which no one is able to shut.'[96]

But someone may object that the door of the gospel is not such an ever-open door: we have a parable of Jesus in which a door is closed as firmly as ever the gates of Jerusalem finally closed on her messianic visitor. In the parable of the Wise and Foolish Virgins people outside beg to have the door opened, and the master of the house refuses their request. You remember how it goes. A village wedding in Palestine, the way the Arabs still celebrate them. None of our bother about clock time. Two separate parties going on all day, one at the bride's house for her family and friends, one at the groom's house for his. Eventually, when the groom is ready, he and his friends go down the street to the bride's house, and then everyone goes back to his place for another party, before all the guests at last go home and leave the happy couple to themselves. The wedding party gets underway only when the guests are going back to the groom's, singing, dancing, banging drums and (since by now it will be night) carrying torches. Some of the bride's friends had been detailed to carry the torches, but not all of them had taken the trouble to make sure they had brought enough oil to pour on the rags. By the time they had remedied things the procession had arrived at the groom's house. The bridegroom was angry with the girls because through their fault the party was not the swinging success it might have been. And so he would have nothing to do with them: he shut the door. Jesus is saying in this parable that easy optimism about our freedom of entry to the life of God will not do. At the crucial moment we may find ourselves unprepared, and that may be the end of everything for us. The door to the City of God cannot be shut by any human hand: but that does not mean to say that men may pass through it carelessly and unnoticing. Suddenly, in the middle of the night, there is the telephone call that demands an immediate response, and on whether or not we make that response in the way the new situation demands of us depends our very selves, our well-being, our integrity, our personality. Our life holds sudden cataracts: the telephone in the middle of the night, the great shout that 'The Bridegroom is here',[97] the trumpet call of God and the voice of the archangel. We imagine that, if we find ourselves unprepared, our friends will help us out, the shops will still be open, and in any case the bridegroom is a fine understanding chap who will hardly lock us out. But he does, he does! Because the girls were unprepared at the critical moment, they lost everything they had been expecting.

The Lenten task in preparation for Easter is to renew our sense of what appropriate steps we might take to be ready for such crucial moments. We have to keep our oil ready, so that by a mere match we can light up everything when these moments befall. We prepare the oil by living as fully as we can in each of the successive moments of ordinary life, by being all there in each different situation. The door of the City of God will only be shut for us if we have not kept it open by a constant going out and coming in, a rhythm and alternation of sensitive response at all the times when the love of God beckons us through the demands of living.

In the Old Testament another Canaanite city, Jericho, was on the defensive against the work of God in history, just as Jerusalem will reject the Saviour later in Holy Week. Jericho was shut up from within and from without: none went out and none came in. Jericho stands as a warning to us about the way we can build up our own defences, stone by stone, day by day and year by year. When out of fear of what might happen to us, of how we might be hurt by other people, we grow a shell and like Jericho turn ourselves into a tortoise, then we become imprisoned and doomed. Normally, it is in the requests of other people to share something of our life that the Lord himself comes to share it. Like the Bridegroom in the Song of Songs he stands knocking at the door, calling on his beloved, his people, to come out and not to wall herself up.

> Jerusalem, Jerusalem, you that kill the prophets and stone those who are sent to you! How often have I longed to gather your children, as a hen gathers her chicks under her wings, and you refused! So be it! Your house will be left to you desolate.[98]

We can watch ourselves with a horrified fascination closing up one door after another in our lives. Very quickly we acquire a reputation for not being available in this way or in that, and then people cease to knock at our door. The urge to self-defence, the urge of Jericho to save itself, is strong in us. But had Jericho opened its gates it would not have been destroyed. Let the whole world march into your heart, the Buchmanites tell us. Jericho, whose doors are barriers, stands in contrast to the new Jerusalem whose doors are means of access. It is those latter doors that are imaged visibly in our churches, whether of the East or of the West. The holy doors of the eastern *iconostasis* both mark out the difference between the Holy of Holies and the nave of the church, and, during the Liturgy, allow the Lord to enter by word and by sacrament. And the doors of a western church on Palm Sunday open as it were spontaneously before the liturgical process, almost like the automatic doors of an airport that open of their own accord as you go forward towards them.

We may say that people take advantage of us, upset us and hurt our feelings. That may well be true. We may indeed have suffered damage from those who abuse our hospitality and our openness. Even so, this is as nothing compared to the damage we will inflict on ourselves if we react by closing ourselves in, by refusing to allow Jesus to be the Door in us. In the first Holy Week the heart of Jesus, which is the house of God and the gate of heaven, was opened on the cross. It will not close on us unless we choose to have it so. In the *Odes of Solomon* Christ is made to say, as he descends into hell:

> I opened doors that were closed,
> and I broke in pieces the bars of iron;
> and the iron became red-hot and melted before me;
> nothing anymore appeared closed to me,
> because I was the Door of everything.[99]

Maundy Thursday: the watching at the Tabernacle

In the Garden of Gethsemane, the disciples whom Jesus takes with him, Peter and James and John, fail to be with him. Again and again Jesus finds them sleeping. He finds that they cannot watch with him one hour. They have that ability, given to some people at moments of great stress, to go to sleep, to withdraw, to be less than present. When the soldiers and the temple police come to arrest Jesus, then all the disciples leave him and flee. At the High Priest's house, when Peter has a chance to be with Jesus again, he denies him three times: he refuses to stand by him. The crowds reject him. The soldiers make mock of him. The people who are crucified with him reject their companionship with him at any deeper level. Jesus is left completely alone. Those whom he might have expected to provide some companionship are not there. The women who had followed him from Galilee and looked after him saw what was going on only from a distance. Luke and John will modify this picture of the complete abandonment of Jesus on the cross. Luke will tell us how one of the other crucified men took his side, and John how there stood by the cross of Jesus Mary his mother and his mother's sister and Mary the wife of Clopas and Mary Magdalen. Neither Luke nor John report Jesus praying the words, 'My God, my God, why have you forsaken me?'[100] But each of the gospels has to be taken in its own right, and we have to be careful not to lose the distinctive message of each by conflating them too quickly. Mark and Matthew report that Jesus is completely abandoned by other people, and that he cries out in the darkness that surrounds him, 'My God, my God, why have you forsaken me?' The person who is abandoned by other human beings, by those whom he should fairly expect to be there to support him at least with their presence, that person can so easily think himself abandoned by God too. As Matthew tells the story, Jesus finds himself in the position of the psalmist. The people who pass by, the chief priests, the scribes, the elders, attack him in the words of the psalm, 'He trusts on God; let him deliver him now if he desires him.'[101] And from that he discovers himself forsaken by God as well. Like the man in another psalm he can say:

> You have put my acquaintances far from me;
> you have made me an abomination to them.
> Lover and friend you have put far from me;
> my one companion is darkness.[102]

And in that darkness he feels himself abandoned by God as well; he has no one. This report we must take with full seriousness, even as we note that the psalmist's faith is so strong that it is not shaken even by the failure to find a hidden and a silent God. He has no one.

One of the saddest texts in all Scriptures is that of the man in St John's Gospel who says to Jesus, 'I have nobody.'[103] There he lies by the side of the healing pool next to the Sheep Gate in Jerusalem. He has been lying there for thirty-eight years. He is more pathetic even than Job on his dunghill. And what he says to Jesus are words like those that any person in one of our hospitals must hear every day, words that any social worker hears again and again: 'I have nobody.' He has nobody to help him get down to the pool at the crucial times when the pool does its healing work. He has nobody to perform little services for him when he needs them. Simply, 'I have nobody.' In that story Jesus ignores all the people round the pool, the people who have someone to help them take advantage of the reserves and resources of healing power that the pool represents. He bypasses what the text speaks of as this 'multitude of those who were sick, blind, halt, withered', and goes straight to the man who has nobody. Why is he so special? Because the Lord himself has so decided things. Because the Word of God in all his freedom chose to be such a man. True, we ought to be able to see the face of Jesus in the face of every one of our fellow men and women; but there are some special people with whom Jesus has particularly identified himself of his own freewill. I was hungry, I was thirsty, I was badly clothed, I was sick, I was in prison. We find Jesus above all, however, in the man who says, 'I have nobody'. Jesus in his dying becomes in particular the person who has nobody, and who having nobody feels himself abandoned by God. The man or woman who has nobody is privileged for Christians, because there is the privileged occasion, the special opportunity, of meeting and serving Jesus. There is the embodiment of Jesus on the cross at what, at least for two of the evangelists, is his final word.

Jesus, then, shares in that loss of God which is death and loneliness. He does not, of course, reject God: he *prays* the psalm of the loss of God. What he loses is all sense of what God had meant to him in the past, of God as he had discovered him and been discovered by him. Corresponding to his praying of this psalm, this word from the cross, is the mystery of his going down into hell, to where, in Old Testament thought, God was not but all mankind was.

That pattern of passing through a dark night, through abandonment by the familiar God, has been not uncommon in the experience of Christians. Angela of Foligno knew it, as did Mechtild of Magdeburg, Henry Suso, John Tauler, Catherine of Siena, Walter Hilton, Rose of Lima. The young Francis de Sales believed that he was damned and sent God a written declaration that he wanted to serve him even in hell. Teresa and John of the Cross describe the experience at some length, and Thérèse of Lisieux lets us know of that underground journey in which she had no idea of where she was going nor of how long it would take. Like Job, Christians have found God to be a disappointment, a puzzle, even an enemy. But like Jesus, they have been prepared to risk a conflict, to come before God and speak with all the boldness and the complaining of this psalm of Jesus on the cross. And this is not, strictly speaking, an experience that is peculiar in certain Christians. Because the descent into hell is a mystery of Jesus himself, a space is opened in which any Christian may be required to stand and live. It may not happen to all of us, but it could happen to any of us.

We are told often enough nowadays that the Church is of its nature missionary, that by our own new nature we share the mission of Jesus and are given his job to do. We are reminded that it is not enough just to stand with Jesus and face the Father, not enough to concern ourselves with our own spiritual wellbeing. To belong to Jesus we must share in the work of Jesus. The Spirit of the Lord has been given to us, especially in Confirmation, for the same reason that it was given to him, so that we can bring good news from God and about God to people who are in need of it – whether by our words or by our deeds. But the pattern of Christian living is the pattern of the life of Christ himself, the one who is in person the good news about God and from God. His pattern of living is offered to us in the gospels so that we can enter into it and it into us, that we may come to have that mind in us which was first in him. Beneath the particular stories of the gospel tradition lie the deep patterns of that life. And these are concerned not only with the coming of Jesus preaching good news or his resurrection from amongst the dead when he was constituted Son of God in power, but also with his prior going down to be amongst the dead, with his God-forsakenness, with his loneliness and his solitude. We have to imitate what is contained in the mystery of Jesus praying the psalm of abandonment and descending into hell, as much as what is comprised in the mystery of the resurrection. We have to be crucified with Christ if we are to rise with him. In Mark's gospel the equivalent to the myth of the descent into hell is the story of Jesus being in the desert. We also have to go into that desert with him, if ever we are to go with him into Galilee, preaching the gospel of God. This is the Lenten quality of our lives, that Lenten quality without which they are unbalanced and insecure, not properly underpinned. What we are about in Lent is seeking the shape of the foundations, the deeper patterns of the Messiah's living and of our living. Jesus in the desert, tempted by Satan, with the wild beasts, with angels waiting on him – that is the beginning of the good news. It is not merely what came first, as a matter of fact, but rather what underlies the good news, its basis and foundation, the background to everything else we will hear about in the gospel.

Why does Jesus go into the desert? Not primarily, as we might think, to escape from the pressures of the world. Not primarily for a time of retreat in the ordinary sense of that word, to recharge his batteries after power has gone out from him in the fight against evil in town and city. Time after time, we find that it is when he has been successful against the forces of evil that he goes back to the desert, not for a rest but so as to face up to the demonic forces in disguised ways, to confront head-on the beasts that come up out of the abyss. 'To this end the Son of God was manifested, that he might destroy the works of the devil,'[104] but to do that he had to face the power of evil not just as that evil which was hurting and destroying others but also as the evil that could have destroyed himself, the temptations against his primary call to live as God's Son. There had to be a trail, a tempting, a testing of strength between Jesus and what could open up a chasm between himself and his Father. On the cross, in the mystery of the psalm of aban-donment, he made trial of that possibility in its strongest form. His

102

retreats to the desert, the times when he went into the mountains alone, these were preliminary skirmishes and testings of the ground.

And we are told at the beginning of Lent each year that we too have to enter into this testing and temptation. We too must face up to the evil which might destroy us. We cannot rest content with trying to remove the effects of evil in our lives or in the lives of other people, important as that is. We have to seek out the desert that God provides for us to be with Jesus there, just as really as we have to share in his work of serving others. With Christ we have to be crucified, to be with him in his desolation and sense of loss of God and distance from God, just as much as we have to be raised with him in the glory of the Father. That is how we learn to put substance into our praying to God as Father, saying Abba with Jesus. Jesus goes through the sense of loss of his God, the Holy One of Israel, and on the other side finds his Father, 'Abba, into your hands I commend my spirit.'[105] All the time the Christian life, and especially the Christian religious life, must have this Lenten and desert quality about it. It must possess this readiness to let the Holy Spirit drive us away from the places of our success to the places where we could fail and be destroyed were it not for the help of God, for the angels who wait on us and give us the nourishment we need. But the angels may not be much in evidence. The desert may be the place where there are only wild beasts for the forty days, only the psalm of abandonment, and where the angels come and minister to us not until the end.

Such a desert can for all of us be both found and constructed. There may well be elements of construction work in our desert; that is what the business of fasting and silence and almsgiving is about. We empty our lives of some of the props we use to hide ourselves from our own barren and hollow hearts. We get rid of some of the more obvious material and social encumbrances to meeting God from our cross. But if, to some extent, we are to construct a desert we must not miss the fact that we all have a desert too. Sometimes people have their desert in very obvious ways. People who live alone can be as much alone in a busy city as they would be in the middle of the Sahara. Such loneliness can be transformed from an evil into the good of solitude. It can be experienced as a desert where certainly there are wild beasts but where equally certainly there is the promise of the help of God. Or there is what we might call 'the sleepless night of the soul', a wilderness that we can shield from us by sleeping pills or that we can decide to enter for our soul's salvation. Again, there will be wild beasts there, ghosts and bogies, but again there will be the help we need from God. There can be that dreadful, awesome, half-past three in the morning feeling when the most devout amongst us is close to utter disbelief. But if our body wants to keep vigil, it is as well to let it and not force it into a false sleep. If our body wants to stay awake, then we may discover something of the experience of abandonment by God; we may find ourselves bearing alone the burdens of many others; we may know a little of the loneliness of those who die in the night. But God is there, although not God as we would like him to be. We have to break through to our own relationship with him, as Jesus did. We have to learn the cost of calling him Father and we have to learn how to commit ourselves into his hands. God has no grandchildren, only children, sons and daughters. The desert will test whether we are sons and daughters of God, as the desert and cross tested Jesus. 'If you are . . . If you are . . . If you are . . .' These experiences will bring us face to face with basic temptations which might destroy us but which we have to overcome if we are to share fully in Jesus' relationship to his Father and then in the work of Jesus. 'I don't know what possessed me', we say. 'I can't think what got into me.' These demons, obsessions and compulsions once bound will become passions and drives that are positively friendly, and a help on the way to God. They can be like the wild beasts that were with Adam in Paradise, like the tamed animals in the lives of Francis of Assisi or Jordan of Saxony. But until they are bound and tamed, they will travel out with us into all our Christian busyness and hollow it out from inside.

The temptation for us all is to avoid the desert, not to run the risk of praying this psalm of loneliness and desolation, to avoid being really on our own, to keep ourselves active (even in the best of good works). But we are invited to have throughout our lives that quality by which we find ourselves again without disguises, without all the escapes from truth that we can so easily take now, in the form of noise and images that destroy our uniqueness. In the desert, on the cross, there is danger. But it is the mark of a mature Christian to court danger, not for thrills or kicks but in order to overcome it. The Lenten quality of our lives prepares us to be renewed in the grace of Eastern baptism. Go into the desert, the Church says each year as Lent begins. Go to the cross. Be ready not only to face the onslaught of the Tempter but go out and track him down, for your own and the world's wellbeing.

Good Friday

'When Jesus therefore had received the vinegar he said, "It is accomplished." And he bowed his head and handed over the spirit.'[106] It is finished. It is fulfilled. It is completed. It is all accomplished. The work which the Father had given him to do has been brought to perfection once and for all. As St John gives us the story it is finished on the cross. There it all comes together. There he is lifted up in glory. There he breathes out the Holy Spirit.

That completion of the work of Jesus on the cross is what we celebrate on Good Friday. For the three days of the Paschal Triduum we celebrate the passing over of Jesus from this world to the Father. For three days, because we need time to celebrate it properly. We need time to enter it with our hearts and our minds. Time to understand it a little better and to love it a little more. Time in which to see the one mystery from different vantage-points.

Jesus passes over from this world to the Father. What does that mean? On Maundy Thursday and Easter Night we are told what it means and we act out that meaning, making it happen so that we can grasp its meaning from the inside. It means, firstly, the Mass and all that the Mass means. That we are shown and that we share in on Maundy Thursday. It means the Eucharist and eucharistic living on our part. It means Jesus saying that it was and is all for us; and it means our laying down our lives for one another, offering ourselves to each other in a love like his on Calvary, like the love of his self-offering in the broken Bread and the poured out wine.

And secondly that passing over of Jesus from this world to the Father means baptism and all that baptism means. That we are shown and share in on Easter Night. We see what Jesus' passover means when we see a man dying in baptism to his old life and rising to a new life which can only be that of Jesus. The image of the risen Jesus is a baptized Christian – which is why sin after baptism is always so wrong. There are many images of Jesus amongst us, but the most significant are those that are alive, each one of the baptized. Jesus passing over means all that baptism and eucharist are, a new life lived by us in love.

Jesus' passing over from this world to the Father took place, however, once for all, in himself and for himself. On the cross, then and there, he said, 'It is accomplished.' Before we can talk about the sacramental gifts to us and before we can experience the quality of his life in us there is what happened once and for all, one Friday afternoon, far away and long ago, on a hill just outside Jerusalem. There is the brute fact that Jesus died, crucified by Roman soldiers. From that hard core of a fact everything else flows and to that everything returns. By that everything stands and falls. True, we are baptized Christians who have passed over from one way of life to another. Still, we know how often we do not live as people who are redeemed but fall back into our old way of life. Yet the fact remains that Jesus was crucified and all our failures and all our downright and deliberate wickedness cannot remove the fact. To it we can return in penitence. True, we are Christians who live from the love there is in the eucharist. Still, we know how often we fail to live eucharistically, fail to lay down our lives for one another, fail even to lay down five minutes of our time for one another. Yet the fact remains that Jesus was nailed to a cross and died when Pontius Pilate was governor of Judaea. There stands that hard fact of history, no matter how we respond to it.

On Good Friday afternoon it is the hard fact of the once-and-for-all death of Jesus that we commemorate and rejoice in. We rejoice in the sheer givenness of his death, in the brute fact that Roman soldiers nailed Jesus down on a couple of pieces of wood and left him there till he died. No matter how much we may love him and serve him, no matter how wholehearted we may be in our devotion, that hard fact is what founds it. No matter how many times we deny him, the fact remains that he was crucified that Friday afternoon. That is why we have such an apparently odd centre of concern in our worship on Good Friday. The Liturgy that day centres around a splinter or so of wood. The relic of the cross, slivers of wood, hard, brute, which we agree by a willing suspension of disbelief to take as a material connection with the once and for all crucifixion, forms the centre-piece of it all. We venerate not some image of the crucified Jesus made according to an artist's imagination and by his skill but wood, the hard fact itself, without which all else founders and in whose absence our goodness and our wickedness are alike without ultimate meaning. You may remember that passion play where the centurion hears the different sounds as his men hammer home the nails into the hands of Jesus. 'Flesh,' he says as he hears the first blow; 'Bone,' as he hears the second; then 'Wood,' as the nail bites into the cross itself. That is what we are shown on Good Friday afternoon: 'Behold the wood of the cross!' How harsh and crude we are on Good Friday. But we know that for at least sixteen hundred years on this day Christians have done just this, venerating bits of wood, harsh, crude and materialistic but the foundation without which nothing else can be said. There is a basic earthiness about Good Friday which comes from the once-and-for-all death of Jesus, from the flesh and blood and bones and sinew and sweat – and wood.

All of us can come to this cross, or creep to the cross, as our medieval ancestors used to say. We can come to it no matter how strong our faith is or how weak, because here we are concerned with a bit of secular history. We can come to the cross no matter how virtuous we are, because there is no virtue worth the name except what comes from the cross. We can come to the cross no matter how negligent we are or how wicked, because the cross stands though we may fall.

But surely we ought to come to it with all the faith and love and devotion we can muster. This is the point of listening first to the Word of God in the Liturgy. We listen to people telling us the story of the crucifixion which is the story of that piece of wood. We listen to people telling us of what Jesus has done for us by dying on the cross, on this wood. And later we shall be offered the sacrament of his dying love as his gift. All this is done in the red vestments of triumph, rejoicing in the victory of the cross. Behold it through the eyes of Scripture and through the sight of prayer and sacrament, but also just look with your own two eyes and see. Just touch it with your lips. Solid wood, as solid as the fact of the death of Jesus and as commonplace as wood like any other. For that reason it is what keeps faith truly Christian, scandalous as it may be to the sensitive and the sophisticated. Come and venerate the wood of the cross. That is the invitation held out to us on the afternoon of Good Friday. And from that solid basis we can go on the following night to the crown of the whole celebration, of the passing over of Jesus from this world to the Father. The night after we can at last meet together for the greatest service of the whole year, that mother of all vigils when we pass over with Jesus.

On the cross as he dies Jesus says, 'It is accomplished.' The cross is the fulfilment of the work which the Father has given him to do. It is the ultimate revelation of his love. It is the conclusive reconciliation of the world with God. The resurrection and the ascension are not an undoing of the cross, but its affirmation. In raising Jesus from the dead into glory the Father 'stands by' the Jesus whom we crucified, true to his word which is the word of the cross. The glorification of Jesus is not a reversal of what happened when Jesus was nailed to the wood but God's assent to it, his acknowledgement that the crucified Jesus is his beloved Son. Jesus now goes up in the world to be made Lord and Messiah. On Ascension Day we shall greet him as the only man with any ultimate authority, the only person whose say-so counts in the end. The cross, however, stands. Jesus is still and always Jesus crucified. There is no going back on the crucifixion. Jesus does not want it undone; God does not want it undone, because it is in looking at Jesus crucified that we see him in focus, brought to a still point. And as we get Jesus in focus so we see through him to the heart of God.

Holy Saturday

From his childhood Jesus would have been familiar with the psalms, with the songs of Israel. If Luke is historically accurate in the picture he paints of the circles in which Jesus was born and spent his early life, then he would have had a special affection for the psalms. They were so very much the prayers of those people we call 'the poor of the Lord', those humble simple people who waited for the consolation of Israel, people like Mary and Elizabeth and Simeon. In such circles the psalms would have been prayed with a degree of personal commitment not always there in the public worship of Israel. And if we can accept the likelihood of this familiarity with the psalms, we can see its effect in the last words of Jesus according to Luke's gospel. 'Into your hands I commend my spirit',[107] a verse from Psalm 31. Rabbinic literature often refers to this psalm verse in connection with prayer in the evening. It recommends that the Jew, before going to sleep, should entrust himself with these words to the mercy of God. In the modern Jewish prayerbook it is found among the night prayers for children. Jesus may well have learned just such a practice as a child and remained faithful to it throughout his life. And now as he was dying, as he was about to fall asleep, he prayed as he had always prayed before going to sleep. 'Into your hands I commend my spirit; you have redeemed me, Lord, you God of truth.'[108]

It is at moments when our strength fails that we especially need access to tradition, to something bigger than ourselves which will mediate God to us. It may be that very much of what we do together in more or less ritualistic ways, often so dull, is there to build up our reserves and to give us a reservoir of feeling and thought to draw on for our moments of greatest need. The Office of Compline has this function in the Church. In Compline we repeat again and again the verse from the psalm which Jesus prayed as his goodnight prayer on the cross. At Compline we sing an antiphon to our Lady that is sung traditionally when people are dying. At Compline we enter into a world of images that will sustain us for more than this one night. They will sustain us when we come to die.

Sleep and death. In the New Testament the words are often interchangeable. Lazarus falls asleep. Stephen falls asleep. Sleep is an image of death, but death can be a sleep. What you have to do in order to die properly is not dissimilar to what you have to do in order to live properly. Learning to go to sleep is part of learning to die. Both begin as an acceptance of merely biological situations – the need of the human organism for periodic sleep and the certainty that the body will eventually die. To accept sleep, to submit to the demands of the body, is part of accepting the way the world is made, taking it as good and very good. To accept sleep is to prepare yourself to accept all those other rhythms whereby our life runs. These time aspects of life are becoming more and more important in modern biology which has learned so much about daily rhythms, found in almost all plants and animals from unicellular algae to man. Innumerable biological clocks beat within us below the level of our consciousness. And these form part of our life in the world before God. We adjust to the rhythm of God by accustoming ourselves to the rhythms of day and night, to our biological make-up.

And death is part of our biological make-up as well. Death can be other than this, a punishment for sin, connoting loss and destruction and a falling away from the living God. But the death of Christ, we say, has destroyed death as this purely negative reality and restored its positive relationship to life. We can learn to accept biological death without making it into the death of sin. We learn what it means to be destined to die, always limited, liable, at risk. We learn that with the awe-inspiring certainty that comes to us all at some point in our lives when we realize for the first time that we ourselves will die, and realize that in the head and the heart. We see the first signs of our approaching death in our living bodies as they cease to renew themselves. As no more teeth grow we realise that one day it will be ourselves we have out and not our teeth. Jesus too had to learn to accept that, and indeed to learn not only that he was to die but to learn how to die. How do we learn to die? By practising dying. How do we practise dying? By going to sleep properly night after night, letting the past day go and saying: 'Into your hands I commend my spirit.' Then we discover that it is not just obedience and acceptance of our biological situation but that

110

we can freely and even gladly choose to fall asleep and to die. It can be a matter not just of necessity but of salvation.

The prayer of Jesus on the cross, his good-night prayer, is given to us each night at Compline so that we can find that such letting-go may do us all the good in the world. You cannot 'go to sleep', you fall asleep, you let go into sleep. If we refuse to relinquish our hold on the day, hanging on grimly to our achievements, whatever they are, we shall lose them in the loss of ourselves. But if we let them go they will be ours to enjoy again tomorrow morning, and in the morning of the Resurrection. 'Anyone who loves his life loses it; anyone who loses his life will keep it for eternal life,'[109] because he will have given it into the hands of the Father where it will be safe and sure. He will keep us, and so we can relax the vigil over our own personality not just for one moment or two, when caught offguard, but for a whole night and then for ever.

'Father!' Jesus prays the goodnight prayer he learned when he was a little boy. But he prays it as he has learned to re-read it, as he has filled it out with his own experience over the course of those thirty-odd years. The psalm verse is originally addressed to Adonai, God of Truth, to the Lord, the faithful God. Jesus has learned to say to God not Adonai but Abba. He initiated his disciples into his own mode of prayer. When you pray, you too, say Abba. The image which sums up supremely Jesus' relationship to God is that of son to father. That word 'son' expresses his total dependence on the Father. He owes his very being as Son to the Father. He has nothing that he has not received. And so he is able to hand everything to the Father in complete confidence, for the Father will make of it what he will. The creed that we use at Mass was drawn up to insist that Jesus is one in being with the Father; but it never departs from the understanding of Jesus as Son, as total receiving. So we speak of Jesus not simply as 'God' but as 'God from God', not just as 'Light' but as 'Light from Light', as 'true God from true God'. In his humanity, in the fact and the manner of his taking our flesh, in the way he lived and still lives as one of us, Jesus translated into human terms what it means for him to be Son from all eternity. What he has is always what he receives from God the Father. Already he has committed into his Father's hands the disciples who believed in his word. And so now that his hour has come with the approaching Passion, he can confidently commend his existence, his life, his spirit into the Father's hands. That 'hour', too, Jesus did not grasp at or force forward. He waited to receive it from the

Father. He realized that time comes towards us. We do not have to rush after it. We can wait for God to give us the right hour.

That is the way of life to which we are called as sons and daughters in the Son of God. We are called to receive from the hands of God whatever he chooses to give us, whatever comes to us by way of the laws of nature or the events of life, and to let ourselves be moulded into true sons and daughters in that way. We are to learn with Jesus how to re-read the psalms in the light of this growing awareness of God as Father, to re-interpret the religious experience of Israel in the light of the breakthrough which Jesus made and into which he initiates us as we call on God as Abba. The psalms give us access to a whole tradition bigger than ourselves. They usher us into a large room where we have space to move, but we do not simply accept them and find our experience of God at second-hand. We come to them as the people we are, with a growing awareness of God in our lives, of how he works in and shapes our lives, conforming us to his Son. That firsthand experience enables us to pray the psalms in a way which is all our own. As W. B. Yeats put it,

> The friends that have it I do wrong
> Whenever I remake a song,
> Should know what issue is at stake:
> It is myself that I remake.[110]

Easter Day

The first thing to be said about the resurrection is that we shall never understand it aright until we see it as one mystery with what we call the Ascension and the pouring out of the Holy Spirit. Easter cannot be understood without Ascension Day and Whitsun. All three make up a single liturgical day for, even if we speak of the *pentecostarion*, the great fifty days, they are the days of Easter Day. In the new Lectionary we listen on Whit Sunday to the story of what happened on Easter evening, on the day of the resurrection. According to St John the risen Jesus appeared to his disciples and breathing on them said, 'Receive Holy Spirit',[111] just as in the Genesis myth God breathed on the clay he took from the earth and man became a living being. The Whitsun gospel, which is also the Easter Day gospel, tells of a new creation in which men are made new men. God breathes into clay, and the dust of the earth realizes its potentiality to be man; man made in the image of God. The risen Jesus breathes into the disorganized and dispirited apostles and man is made in the image of Jesus, the new man.

The risen Jesus is the human face of the only God there is. The radical monotheism of the Jewish–Christian tradition has, extraordinarily, this human face and human form. The one and only God there is is bodied forth in the risen Jesus of Nazareth. This risen Jesus breathes out Holy Spirit so that his spirit may become ours, the deepest layer of our personality, and so that thereby we may become sharers in the divine nature. When we celebrate Easter we are celebrating the fact that the whole story of this Jesus is for our salvation. It is for our health, our well-being, our wholeness, our holiness, our realization of all the potentialities we have as human beings made from the dust of the earth. The clay of the ground as the Bible calls it, the hydrogen atom, as we might say scientifically, has the potentiality to be vegetable and then animal and finally human animal, a talking, singing, dancing, music-making animal.

113

But beyond that the hydrogen atom, the dust of the earth, has the potentiality to become divine. We, who are dust of the earth, have the breath of the risen Jesus breathed into us and thereby dust is refashioned into the image and likeness of the body of God. The one Day of Easter is the feast of man's divinization, our becoming sons and daughters in the one Son of God who was made man as Jesus of Nazareth so as never more to be unmanned. The spirit of this particular man is to become our spirit, and it is his image and likeness that we are to take on.

What is his likeness? 'He showed them his hands and his side,' the Easter gospels say; or 'see my hands and my feet;' or, 'Handle me and see'.[112] The risen Jesus is the bruised man, the man with the wounds. He bears in his body the marks of judicial execution, of rejection to the uttermost. The crucifixion is not, in the mind of the gospel writers, a ghastly mistake which God reversed in the resurrection. On the cross Jesus was tempted: 'Come down from the cross if you are the son of God!'[113] He did not succumb to that temptation on the third day. The resurrection confirms the crucifixion and hence Easter faith glories in the cross of our Lord Jesus Christ. Paul, and New Testament Christians in general, actually boast that their Lord was crucified, executed as a criminal. The bruised and battered Jesus with the wounds is the Jesus of Easter, the Jesus of the Ascension and the Jesus of Pentecost, the one who draws all things to himself. From the side of the finite, the highest point of creation is this man with the ever-open wounds. From the side of the infinite, the for-ever crucified Jesus is the translation and embodiment of the only God. Christians are people who say that the only God there is is bruised and wounded; he has an ever-broken heart; he loves and is hurt because he loves. Because on the cross Jesus went on loving God and us, the resurrection can only be the endorsement and vindication of what happened there, not its undoing. In celebrating Easter we celebrate the joy that the cross has brought to the world, since nothing now can separate us from the love of God which is in Christ Jesus our Lord. In celebrating Easter we rejoice in the fact that Jesus still comes to disciples and breathes out on them his Holy Spirit to be our very own.

The love which Jesus showed on the cross is the expression of God not only to us but to all the world, to the light-years of interstellar space. In this perspective the fathers of the Church delighted to see the cross everywhere, the Spirit of the crucified Jesus filling the whole earth. They saw the cross in the body of every man, in the wings of flying birds, in the sails of a ship, in the scales in the market-place. John Donne sums up the patristic tradition for us:

> Who can deny me power, or liberty
> To stretch mine arms, and mine own cross to be?
> Swim, and at very stroke thou art thy cross.
> The mast and yard make one, where seas do toss.
> Look down, thou spiest out crosses in small things.
> Look up, thou seest birds raised on crossed wings.[114]

Resurrection is the fact that the bruised man still comes to us to make us anew in his image by his Spirit. The more we are re-made in his image the more readily will we recognize his presence in all places and at all times, seeing the hanged man with the open wounds everywhere, *his blood upon the rose*. The Christian is not the only man who is present to the crucified Jesus. Rather, he is the man who is beginning to love like him, that Christ who loves people without demanding a return, for he loves for better, for worse and will not cease to love others no matter what they make of his love.

On Good Friday people rejected Jesus, refusing to credit that a man like that, a man who could be killed like that, could possibly be the last word there was to be said about the world. But God repeated the single Word he had spoken. He insisted on it. He was utterly emphatic that Jesus was the ultimate truth about us all. God said it no longer in a provisional way but now in such a way that he made it clear he would never go back on his word. That is what Easter is. God repeats the same word which is the living Jesus Christ, but this time he speaks it as emphatically as he can. He gives his approval to Jesus by glorifying his wounds rather than healing him and removing his scars. His way of life is from now on the most authoritative in the world. All authority in heaven and on earth belongs to him.

And what way of life is that? Jesus is an outgoing person, as Paul says in that famous hymn which he inserted into the Letter to the Philippians. He 'emptied himself'.[115] He does not cling and grasp. He went all out for us, even to the death of the cross. In Jesus God gave himself away in both senses. He revealed the secret of what kind of God he is, and he gave away all that he has to give us. This continues to be the way with Jesus, the way which is Jesus. In the Eucharist there is 'my Body given for you', given in its entirety.

115

This, we say, is the mystery of faith, the revelation of God giving himself away. But this mystery, this revealed reality, is visible only to the eyes of faith. It was only in the sight of the apostles whom he had chosen that Jesus was lifted up. Those who can see that his is the authority of the 'author' of a new humanity have the task of trying to make that authority more apparent. Christians try to let that authority of the crucified and risen Christ appear through the way they are. Their task and mission is to encourage others to follow the way which is Jesus. But before this can happen they must first make their lives a complete giveaway of God. They must become themselves self-emptying people, outgoing people, people who go all out for others.

Prayer before the Blessed Sacrament fits here. Eucharistic adoration is looking to Jesus in that complete giveaway which is the Sacrament of his Body and Blood, the true body born of Mary, the body that truly suffered and was killed on the cross, himself and not another. The solidity of our faith in the Eucharist depends on the truth that it is himself. The gospels make this point by telling us of the emptiness of the tomb on Easter morning. It may, and will, take much loving thought and prayer to enter into the mystery of the resurrection but there is one necessary condition for resurrection. The grave was empty, the body gone. Whatever marvellous things there are to say about Easter could be instantly discounted if the corpse could be produced. There is no such thing as a non-bodily resurrection except as a metaphor, a way of talking. Even then, the metaphor is grounded in the more primary concept of the raising of the body. The Word of God who became flesh in Jesus of Nazareth had a passion for the physical, for humanity as it really is. He had a passion, a suffering, a death for it. Jesus had his passion not so that we should forget that we are dust but so that we should be glad and exult in that fact. The psalmist says that God himself remembers that we are dust, and in Scripture to remember always means to do something about a thing. God, remembering that we are dust, shares our dust by becoming flesh and has a passion for it so that our dust may be transformed, transfigured and glorified. The risen Jesus whom we adore in the Blessed Sacrament is the Jesus who has had that passion which is suffering and death, as well as that passion which is love, for our dust. What happens in the resurrection and in the transformation of the eucharistic Gifts is so marvellous and so unforeseeable that we cannot stop short of calling it a new creation; and yet it is really a recreation of what

already is. If the corpse were still rotting in the grave, if the Eucharist we worship had no continuity with the bread which is the work
of our hands, then we would be able to ignore or despise our bodies
and all that is bodily about us: our hunger and thirst, our sexuality,
all the nexus of human relationships, personal and social. We could
treat the world as a mere distraction, had the grave not been empty.
The material world with its sorrows and joys might be simply
obstacles to our prayers, were the body still in the tomb. Because
the tomb is empty, because the Blessed Sacrament is the true flesh
and blood of Jesus, we cannot ignore the world or reject it. We can
only love the world that God so loved. We can only hope to deepen
our passion for the world for which Jesus had such a passion. When
we say, Christ is risen, we mean that he, the embodied person and
not some ghost, has risen and that the wounds of the Crucified have
eternal significance for all our human endeavour.

Easter: The second Sunday[116]

When Jesus appears to the eleven disciples he says to them, 'Look at my hands and my feet, that it is I myself,'[117] and he shows them his hands. When they saw those hands he was holding out to them a whole host of memories must have come flooding back. The gospel tradition is full of references to the hands of Jesus. Mark continually invites us to see Jesus putting his hand into the hand of people in need, just as the Father in the Old Testament was said to stretch out his arm to save. He takes Simon's mother-in-law by the hand and raises her up from her fever. He takes the blind man by the hand at Bethsaida. He takes the epileptic boy by the hand and raises him up when people thought he was dead. We see him stretching out his hand to touch the leper and laying his hands on sick people at Nazareth to heal them. We find him taking children in his arms and blessing them, again with the gesture of laying on hands. We watch him touch the tongue of the deaf man who had an impediment in his speech and putting his finger in his ear so that the man's ears were opened and so that he spoke clearly. Matthew tells us how he stretched out his hand to save Peter from drowning. And, given 'the mighty works worked by his hands,' it is hardly surprising that people ask Jesus to use his hands, those life-giving, creative, healing hands. Other people bring him the deaf man and ask him to lay his hand on him. Other people bring the blind man to him and ask him to touch him. Other people bring little children for him to touch.

The hands of Jesus also cover the space between his death and his risen life, his life with people in the time of the Church. At Mass, when we are praying the Roman Canon, we say that Jesus took bread in his holy and venerable hands. Other catholic liturgies share this interest in the hands. They speak of his holy and blessed and pure hands, or those hands with which he formed the world. They refer to his life-giving hands or to those hands which were to

118

be pierced for us. Yet curiously enough none of the New Testament accounts of the Last Supper specifically mention the hands of Jesus. The liturgies are original here, surely because their makers had something of that delight in thinking of the Lord's hands that we have in looking at the skilled hands of a surgeon or a pianist, or the wrinkled hands of our grandmother, or the earthy hands of a farmer. At Mass we are invited by this recalling of the hands of Jesus at one of the central moments in the eucharistic prayer, to activate our own gospel memories of the hands of Jesus, those hands which translate into terms of flesh and blood the hands of God the Father. At the moment in the eucharistic prayer when we remember before God all that Jesus said and did at the Last Supper, all the mighty works done by the hands of Jesus are concentrated. And equally, in that moment and in the result of that moment, held as it is in the eucharistic Presence, all the love and the power in the hands of Jesus are made available to us.

We see the love and the power, the care and the compassion in, for instance, the stories of Jairus' daughter and the woman with the haemorrhage Jesus met on the way to the house of Jairus. The synagogue official comes to Jesus and asks him to lay his hands on the little girl. He does so, taking her by the hand and raising her up. Whenever we come to communion we are invited to let that compassion and love of Jesus flow into us so that we may be raised up as well into something new. All that loving power of Jesus is made available for us if we will take it. 'Take,' Jesus says, 'Take and eat, take and drink.' Each time the gospel is read at Mass it is read so that it can happen again. The style in which Christians have 'taken' the power and love and compassion, made visible and tangible in the Bread and Wine, has differed widely. Nowadays the option has been restored to us of taking what the Lord offers in the way our fathers in the faith took it in the golden age of Christianity, that is, by reaching out our hands for the gifts of God to be put into them. It is only an option: we must not make too much of particular ways of doing things. But we must not make too little of different ways either. To stretch out one's hands for Holy Communion involves a whole spirituality, a whole relationship to God and the things of God. For what we do with our hands is never insignificant. Quintillian, writing about A.D. 80 in his *Institutio Oratoria* says other portions of the body merely help the speaker, whereas the hands may almost be said to speak themselves. Do we not use them to demand, promise, summon, dismiss, threaten, supplicate, express

119

aversion or fear, question or deny? Do we not use them to indicate joy, sorrow, hesitation, confession, penitence, measure, quantity, number and time? Have they not the power to excite and prohibit, to express approval, wonder or shame? Do they not take the place of adverbs and pronouns when we point at places and things? In fact, though the people and nations of the earth speak in a multitude of tongues, they share in common the universal language of hands. The hands of the Father are eloquent hands, and we see what they say in the hands of Jesus. In turn we commend ourselves into those hands, by stretching out our own hands to take all they offer us. To use this particular sacramental gesture should never degenerate into a meaningless movement. In fact it can never so degenerate. If it does become a casual and slipshod gesture that itself has its meaning. It speaks eloquently of our lack of concern for the things of God.

Like the woman with the haemorrhage we reach out our hands to touch the Lord, our hand answering to his hand, like the finger of God and the finger of Adam reaching for one another in the Michelangelo fresco. To the life-giving, healing, creative hands of Jesus answer our hands as we come empty-handed and open-handed, ready to receive with both hands whatever he wishes to give us on this occasion. All his care and compassion and power and concern are focussed in the Bread and the Cup which he took in his holy and venerable hands. All our need for him and our readiness for him are brought to a point in our open hands, reaching out to touch him. That is the way we commit ourselves into the hands of the Father; by taking whole-heartedly all that he gives. 'Hold Infinity in the palm of your hand,' says Blake; and that particular way of going to Communion takes that close to the letter. People who adopt this style of communicating are hearing the words of the Lord of the conspicuous scars to Thomas: 'Reach your finger here and see my hands.'[118] Reach out your hand. They rediscover his words to the Eleven in the upper room on Easter evening, 'Handle me and see.' With St John they can talk not only of what they have heard and what they have seen with their eyes but also of what their hands have handled of the Word of life. Like the woman with the haemorrhage, they have heard the things about Jesus, and they reach out their hand to be healed of whatever in their lives needs healing. So it can be at Communion like those other gospel scenes that Mark describes. Wherever Jesus went, they asked him if they might touch just the fringe of his garment. And everyone of those who touched him was made whole.

But in the end, it is our faith that saves us. Whichever way we come ritually to Communion, kneeling or standing, open-handed or open-mouthed, what matters is the faith with which we approach. The crowd was jostling Jesus, says Augustine; the woman touched him. What does 'touched' mean? Simply, 'believed'. What sort of faith must we have at our fingertips or on the tip of our tongue if communion is to be effective? What kind of faith must there be if we are to put ourselves into the hands of Jesus, and so into his Father's hands from which no one can snatch us? Faith like that of Jairus and the woman with the haemorrhage. Faith that the healing power of Jesus is there for us. Faith that he can make new things happen in our lives even at times when everything is grinding to a halt. It is not a question of resigning ourselves to the will of God but of accepting our 'hour' from his hand. We commend our life into the hands of God by taking into our own hands whatever it is that God gives.

Easter: the third Sunday[119]

Why is it, ultimately, that we celebrate Easter? It is not because we are temperamentally convinced of the inherent goodness of the world, as if it simply lay within our nature to affirm that goodness of creation of which the Book of Genesis speaks. Nor do we keep Easter because we are incurable optimists and, as dreamers of dreams ourselves, love to hear the dream imagery of others. Nor, again, do we keep Easter because of a promise by God that at some point in the future he will forgive us and renew us. In other words, our keeping of Easter is not parasitic on Genesis or Isaiah or Ezekiel. On the contrary, it is Judaism that depends on Christianity. The words of the prophets come alive, leaping out from the printed page, only when they are read in the light of the paschal candle which burns on our sanctuaries throughout the Easter season. We keep the Easter season only because of what happened once in the middle of a spring night in a garden just outside Jerusalem. We keep the Easter season only because God has raised Jesus from the dead – and if Christ be not risen, then is our faith vain, and our preaching vain, and we are still in our sins, and of all men the most to be pitied. Without the moment of the resurrection our keeping high holiday in springtime is nothing but a charade, a natural festival in thin disguise.

When Jesus died the Old Testament died too, and was buried with him. 'We *had* hoped,' the Emmaus travellers say, speaking in the most definite of past tenses. But the earth had reeled and rocked; the whole established order had swayed; any goodness they might have seen in the world was negated when Herod and Pilate between them destroyed their hopes. Amazingly, the world still went on, but it was a changed world. Things and persons now seemed shadowy rather than substantial. The world was only too palpably poised over chaotic deeps that could rise up at any moment and overwhelm it. Their own lives were suspended over a threatening and perilous void. Any order could only be temporary now, and all accepted rules and standards uncertain in their application. The high hopes of the Old Testament were buried, and with them the abiding word of any mighty acts which God might have done for his people in the past. What certainty was there, God having sent his only Son when so many messengers had been turned back, and that Son now himself a murdered man, that he would not abandon his people and his world to their own folly? Had not Jesus himself threatened that Jerusalem would be destroyed?

'We *had* hoped that it was he.' But perhaps those hopes of the disciples were about to be realized, and realized today. In its own way, that is at least as frightening a prospect as the fear that they would not be realized at all. It is not kind to bring human anticipations to a close too suddenly and dramatically. We all possess some sort of hope for the future, some dream of how things will turn out. We need this for healthy living. The hopes of the disciples had been shattered. How marvellous if they could be given hope again in their dark night! But how terrifying if, instead of hope, they were given the realization of their hopes today, this very day. The moment that people surmise that perhaps something altogether unexpected has happened, so that they are required not so much to pick up the pieces of their old life as to become involved in something quite new and staggering, then they are afraid. The accounts of the resurrection appearances in the New Testament are full of such fear. In Luke's gospel, Jesus comes in amongst the eleven disciples just after the travellers on the Emmaus road have reached Jerusalem. He greets them with the word 'Peace', but they are terrified. The Church, too, begins her celebration of Eastertide in the middle of the night, surrounded by the darkness with its shapes and sounds, the everyday objects of our experience strangely altered in the paschal moonlight. If we took the resurrection seriously would we really be as glad as we are when the light is struck from the flintstone and the Easter bonfire goes roaring up to the sky? In the person of the priest we take a knife in our hands to carve the name of Christ, and his claim on this year as on all years, in the wax of the paschal candle. But how easily the knife might slip; and we were always warned how dangerous it is to play with fire. The Eastertide which begins on Easter night is in one sense a fearful time, for it demands something from us not tomorrow but now, today.

And yet how simple, how human it all is. We can let the fear of

123

panic go, even if the fear of reverence has to remain and permeate our whole lives. Jesus 'appeared' to his disciples at various times, we are told, and in various ways. Rather, what the evangelists normally say is that he 'showed himself' to his disciples after he had been raised from the dead. Before Jesus was killed it was up to you whether you saw him or not. All you had to do was to go out and look for him, and if you found him, you saw him. But from Easter onwards, it was up to the Lord himself to let you see him. What we have in the stories in the last chapters of the gospels is how he did in fact 'show himself' to others. For forty days, a shortish period of time and a good round number (like the forty days) we keep between Easter Day and the feast of the Ascension, he showed himself in the ways and at the times he chose. Nobody ever saw him again like that, after those few extraordinary weeks of spring-time in Palestine so long ago. Whatever we may mean by 'the ascension' it must at least mean that. We cannot hope to see the Lord in the way those men and women involved in the Resurrection appearance saw him. They saw someone they had known for three or four years past, subtly different in all manner of ways from before yet still recognizably the same. After those few short weeks that unique period of history was over and done with. But not quite. The people who narrated these stories did not do so because they happened, although they did happen. What is happening in all these incidents which will never happen again in the way they happened then is that Jesus is offering us a kind of identikit of himself. Since the Ascension Jesus has gone incognito, and these stories give us a hint of how to penetrate his disguise.

The travellers on the Emmaus road did not divine the identity of the risen Lord until they had stopped just listening and started practising, and offered him their active hospitality. They did not recognize him until his actions spoke louder than his words as he took bread and gave thanks over it and broke it and gave it to them. People like these, the familiars of Jesus, could check that their identification was right, by looking at his hands, or his wounded side, or whatever. We can no longer do that. All we have to go on are these stories about the ways in which Christ has chosen to mask his presence, so that when we come across the tell-tale signs we shall know who is really there.

Take the story of the disciples going fishing (an alternative gospel text for this Sunday in the Church's Lectionary). This story serves to break the smooth pattern of things arranged in sevens in John's gospel, a pattern which was his way of expressing the fulfilment of all things in Christ, but which so easily could leave us with the sense of it all being over and complete, merely to be admired and wondered at. But then, tagged on to the apparent end, we have this extra story about the disciples going about their daily business. To single out one aspect of this workaday story, notice the invitation of Jesus, 'Come and have breakfast'. 'Now none of the disciples dared to ask, "Who are you?" They knew it was the Lord.'[120] The disciples recognize the Lord in the man who stands there offering them hospitality, refreshing them with just what they need after a heavy night's fishing. Here we have one of the incognitos of the risen Jesus. We are so used to being told to recognize the Lord in the poor and the sick and in those who are suffering in any way, in the tramp at the back door and the guest in the parlour. That is right and proper and evangelical. Wherever people are suffering and oppressed there the Lord most surely is in the person of those who suffer; and our task is to do what we can to serve him there, caring for him in their needs which are his needs. But it is not the only incognito presence of Christ. He is really present too whenever it is we ourselves who are being helped, whenever people care for us in the most homely and everyday ways such as the invitation to have breakfast. We need to learn that we have to be not only givers, generous and outoing, but also receivers, those who will let other people do things for us, albeit homely and everyday things. If we refuse the help and kindness of others we refuse the Lord himself, present among as one who serves. He says that at the banquet in his kingdom he will be the servant, donning an apron as he did at the Last Supper in order to wait on us at table. How hard it is for independent people such as ourselves to learn that lesson. When we grow old it is even harder because we have been so active and independent throughout our lives. But it gives joy to the heart of the risen Lord if we let him wait on us, making our bed, sweeping our floor, bringing up a tray to our room at teatime. As the tree falls so will it lie. Whilst we still have our strength and vigour, we must begin to practise the art of letting others help us, not getting crotchety, for instance, when we are out of sorts for a few days and people fuss around us.

No matter how many times we have denied the Lord we will have the same number of opportunities to express our love for him. Peter found out as much that spring morning by the lakeside in those three questions of Jesus to match the three questions of the

125

enemies of Jesus which had led him to deny his Lord. He had missed his opportunities in the past: he took them now, quietly, humbly. At the supper in the upstairs room he had tried to stop the Lord waiting on him; now he accepted the Lord's service with gratitude.

Easter: the fourth Sunday[121]

As Moses was preparing to hand over the leadership of Israel to Joshua he spoke of a time when 'the Lord your God will raise up for you a prophet like myself from among your brethren'. Later on in the saga of Israel's dealings with her God, God's fundamental promise to David was the promise of a son in whom David's house and kingdom would be made sure for ever. Even within the lifetime of Jesus there were those who considered that these prophecies had been fulfilled in the rabbi from Nazareth, that he was the expected prophet, and that it was right to welcome him into David's city with the words, 'Hosanna to the Son of David.'[122] After his resurrection it seemed even more appropriate to speak of Jesus in terms issuing from the stories of Moses and of David. Now each of those two crucial Old Testament figures had fulfilled the role of shepherd. Both of them, in the first place, had been literal shepherds, caring for their sheep in desert and on hillside. Both of them, secondly, were called to be shepherds of their people. The concept was not, however, limited to Israel. Speaking of a king or leader as his people's shepherd seems to have been a very common way of talking about political leadership in the ancient Near East. The reason is not far to seek. Societies formed by sheep are like most human societies: stupid, affectionate, gregarious, easily stampeded, wanting a leader and lost without one. And so it seemed appropriate enough that, just as the Pharoahs had been called shepherds of their people, just as the rabbis spoke of Moses as the compassionate Shepherd, just as David had been called to shepherd Israel, so Jesus should be called shepherd too, the Good Shepherd, or, literally, the Beautiful Shepherd. The title as placed on the lips of Jesus suggests a hint of argumentation. '*I* am the Lovely Shepherd,' *I* rather than someone else.

Jesus claims to be the one who really satisfies our hunger for someone to shepherd us, to lead us, to give us a sense of belonging.

127

In the East the relationship between shepherd and sheep is different from the relationship with which we are familiar. In the East sheep are kept for their milk and wool, not as a source of mutton. The shepherd and his sheep, therefore, may be together for as long as eight or nine years. Each shepherd has his own peculiar call which his sheep recognize and follow. He goes first, leading his sheep into places where he knows it is safe for them to go; and in this procession each sheep receives a name. How often the Shepherd of Israel calls each person by his name: Abraham, Abraham; Moses, Moses; Saul, Saul. Jesus affirms, then, that he is personally that shepherd he speaks of in the parable of the lost sheep. Because he is shepherd other people can afford to count themselves among the sheep of the gospel metaphor. While we normally think of sheep in pejorative terms there is something in the character of a sheep which might be worth imitating – the virtue of non-assertiveness. Wanting to be someone, to count and to cut a figure in the world is an altogether fundamental human need, as basic as the need for food or drink, or shelter or clothing from the cold. It is the need to *be* somebody, and without its fulfilment it is doubtful if we shall constitute a person at all. This affair of being somebody is termed by Scripture 'glory' or 'weight', in the sense we speak of a person making a weighty intervention in some debate. We all want this weightiness: we all need to count for something. But if Jesus is the glory of Israel, then he shows us a way of having glory which does not involve being aggressive and fighting for it. We can enjoy personal weight in the world not by our ability to dominate others but by placing the way we matter outside of ourselves, in the glory of being disciples, or sheep, of the good Shepherd. We can renounce all violent grasping at glory. We can let down those defensive high walls through which nobody goes out and nobody comes in. We do not need now to wield our anger like a sword. We can cease holding one another up to ransom by our moods. We can be content to be sheep, defined in relation to our glorious Good Shepherd.

And yet we also have to be shepherds. There is no contradiction in this. Once again, it is the way of Jesus, implied in the task of growing up in all things into Christ who is our Head. Shepherding is a ministry in the Church by the human will of the historical Jesus himself. Some people are so much involved in a permanent way in this ministry that they are known simply as pastors, 'shepherds' in English. But, as with so many forms of service in the Church, they really bring to a point and make obvious and total what must be

128

an aspect of the Christian lives of us all. All of us have some sort of obligation to care for others. Such concern may well include that kind of activity that Israel's shepherds found themselves engaged in, the guarding of the flock, even to the point of the destruction of its enemies. Christ is not just a mild shepherd-lad piping down the valleys wild, sitting under the shade of the trees at noon. David said to Saul:

> Your servant used to keep sheep for his father; and when there came a lion or a bear and took a sheep from the flock, I went after him and smote him and delivered it out of his mouth; and if he arose against me, I caught him by the beard, and smote him and killed him.[123]

The second David is often presented in early Christian art as just such another, one who smites the lion and the bear. As Christ the Conqueror he wins the victory over the non-human forces that threaten his people, trampling on the dragon and the basilisk, those forces of chaos which the Book of the Apocalypse describes in terms of beasts rising up out of the sea. A balanced theology cannot escape integrating the place of the demons into its picture of existence. The Bible and the Church accept the common experience of mankind that between man and God is a realm which is neither human nor divine, the realm of principalities and powers. These powers can and do threaten the life of man, for, while in principle good, they fall and become snares and delusions. According to the Book of the Apocalypse, the great dragon, 'that ancient serpent who is called the Devil and Satan',[124] lay undisturbed in heaven until the woman had given birth to her Child, until Israel in Mary had given birth to the Messiah who, like a shepherd, was to rule the nations; and until that Christ-child had been lifted up to God and his throne, until Jesus was crucified and raised. There is now no place for a Satan, an Accuser, a prosecution lawyer, in heaven. Not without a struggle he was expelled, and with him all the ideas and laws and national spirits that insist with Satan on the principle of merciless just deserts. We too share in that struggle and victory of the strong Shepherd, that war in heaven.

In the Byzantine Church, the epistle for the Mass of monastic clothing tells the novice that he 'must have his loins girded with truth, putting on the breastplate of righteousness, equipped with the gospel of peace on his feet . . . donning the helmet of salvation

and taking up the sword of the Spirit, which is the word of God'.[125]
The arms of the gentle, but the arms of those who have to fight. As
so often, the monk stands for the whole Church. We are told that
we are 'contending not against flesh and blood, but against the
principalities and powers, against the world rulers of this present
darkness, against the spiritual hosts of wickedness in the air'.[126]
This includes all those social forms and dogmas which constitute
fate for so many people, those tyrants of the market-place and the
home, the worship of the national spirit, the traditions which fall
and become inflexible conventions or, worse still perhaps, compla-
cencies, and those insidious authorities of unreason and passion
that speak through propaganda and the mass-media. These are the
false gods that we sing about in the psalms and mock. To fight
against the demons who live in the atmosphere is to fight for a
human world, a world in which the man-child is on the throne, a
world where economic and social and psychological laws are subject
to us and serve us and do not lord it over us. It means trying to
find ways of breaking through inevitabilities, ways of turning the
other cheek – that gesture whose success depends on the fact that
it is so totally unexpected a thing to do. The demons win when they
present themselves as inevitabilities: then they hold us fast in the
grip of their past and make it our own. To fight the demons is to
fight for the reality of forgiveness, for the gospel message that new
beginnings are possible, for the power of absolution.

Jesus the Good Shepherd, then, expels the demonic from where
God is, when he enters heaven. According to a common patristic
exegesis, in entering heaven he is bearing on his shoulders the lost
sheep of the human race, for whose sake he left the ninety-nine
choirs of angels in the fold and came seeking the one that had
strayed. The ascension of Jesus, in other words, re-integrates creation, re-uniting man and the angels. Already, according to the
Pauline epistles, we are not only crucified with Christ but we have
risen with him, and with him we are already seated at the right
hand of God. 'Those who are accounted worthy to attain to the age
to come and to the resurrection from the dead are . . . equal to
angels and are sons of God, being sons of the resurrection.'[127] In
this quotation from Jesus, Luke modifies Mark's version of the text,
toning down its futurist language. Life in fellowship with the angels
can be experienced here and now. Man is now once again, as
Gregory of Nyssa says, in the dancing ranks of the angelic spirits,
through the work that Jesus, the Good Shepherd, has accomplished.

Man is made for festivity. He is a being *à la Mozart*. If we refuse to be festive, shunning such good things as come our way in life, we are saying that we would rather that Jesus had not become the Good Shepherd. He may be the Shepherd but there is nothing lovely, beautiful, charming about such a shepherd in our eyes. Whereas to accept festivity, to be able to laugh, is to allow that he has indeed done all things well.

Easter: the fifth Sunday[128]

Jesus of Nazareth tells us that he comes not to destroy the law, the past, but to fulfil it. He comes to fulfil the faith of Abraham and the law of Moses, the promises to David and the hopes of the prophets, and the expectations of Israel. He tells us that he is in a new and definitive manner all the gifts that God had given to his people in the past: Bread of Life like the desert manna; the Good Shepherd, like her leaders; the Way, like the way home from exile; the Truth, like her own possession of God's self-revelation. He tells us too that he is all that God had promised his people in the future: the Resurrection and the Life, and what Israel was to be for all nations, the Light, a light to the whole world. But in the end he claims to be not only what Israel had been given or promised or was meant to be among men, but that he is in some way Israel herself. I am the true Vine, he says. In the Psalms we sing:

> God brought a vine out of Egypt;
>   he drove out the nations and planted it;
> The mountains were covered with its shade,
>   the mighty cedars with its branches;
> It sent out its branches to the sea,
>   and its shoots to the Great River Euphrates.[129]

Jesus alleges that he is personally that vine, all who believe in him being its branches, and its vinedresser being his Father, the Lord, the God of Israel.

From early times this image caught on in the Church. In the *Didache*, a book of the early second century, we have a prayer which reads:

We give thanks to you, our Father, for the Holy Vine of David,

132

your son and servant, which you made known to us through Jesus your Son and Servant; glory to you for ever.[130]

This prayer falls within a series of prayers for the Eucharist. 'Concerning the Eucharist,' the rubric goes, 'concerning the prayers of thanks, give thanks thus. First, concerning the cup.' And then follows the prayer just cited. For obvious reasons, Jesus' words about himself as the true Vine found an echo in Eucharistic prayers over the cup which contained the fruit of the vine. The *Didache* is especially close in this to the Gospel of St John. In the Fourth Gospel there is no account of Jesus' words over the bread and wine at the Last Supper. Instead, John gives us a story about how Jesus took a towel and washed his disciples' feet, serving them in the most humble way possible. This story is meant to indicate one of the central truths about the Eucharist: in the Eucharist Jesus sums up his whole life as a life of service, service which we must imitate if we are to share his life. John is no anti-sacramentalist, no primitive Quaker. He has much to say to us about the Bread and the Cup, but he says it outside the context of the Supper itself. What he has to say about the Eucharistic Bread comes early in the gospel, in that long speech of Jesus on the occasion of the feeding of the five thousand, a speech similar to the explanatory discourse of the Jewish paterfamilias at Passover. (There are even four questions asked, as at Passover.) It is not quite true to say, however, that this chapter is about the Eucharistic Bread. What is the case is that both the Eucharistic Bread and this chapter are about Jesus as the Bread of Life, the one who offers himself for our nourishment in a variety of ways, but most typically in the Eucharist. What John has to say about the Wine of the Eucharist comes in his chapter about the True Vine. Once again, the visible word of the sacrament and the word of Scripture both speak to us of the same reality, the reality which lies beyond all our telling. This reality comes to expression in, but is never exhausted as, the word spoken of in Scripture and the word celebrated in the sacrament. The personal Word of God, Jesus of Nazareth, is attainable only as the word of man, as the audible word and the visible word. We encounter him as the word of our words and of our actions, as we minister him to each other in pouring out the wine-cup and sharing it. Jesus is the Word of God beyond all telling, yet we are in duty bound to tell his story; and in that telling he comes to us, to remain with us and to enable us to remain, to abide, with him. We spell out what he is in human

133

words and human gestures. We speak about the true Vine and its Vinedresser, its branches and its fruit. And we take the fruit of the vine, pour it out, give thanks to God and over it and share in that cup together. These words and gestures bring to expression the one reality which is Christ, the Vine which is Israel and the new Israel, the Vine whose fruit makes glad the heart of man.

In the desert Moses had promised the old Israel: 'The Lord your God is bringing you into a good land, a land of brooks of water, of fountains and springs, a land of wheat and barley and of vines.'[131] But there were always those in Israel for whom the Promised Land seemed a mixed blessing. There were those who always held out for Israel being fundamentally a desert people, a pilgrim people. Nazarites and Rechabites made their protests against the settlement of the people of God by having nothing to do with the vine or its products. They protested against civilization by abstaining from that most civilized and most humanized plant, the vine. They enacted their statement that what God had given to his people was too dangerous, and ought to be avoided. For Christians who belong to the era of the incarnation, when God entered the realm of matter, there can be no such doubting of the essential goodness of things, no kind of wish or suggestion that it would be better if they did not exist. We have to drink of the fruit of the vine, and unless we drink of the fruit of the true Vine, we have no life in us.

More than that, we have in a sense to become wine for others, offering ourselves to them as the Vine's own fruit. 'I am the Vine, you are the branches. He who abides in me and I in him, he it is who bears much fruit.'[132] And so Augustine can say, 'There are you in the chalice!'[133] We stretch out our hands for the Eucharistic Bread, the Body of Christ, and find that we are receiving the mystery of what we ourselves are, his Body. Similarly in stretching out our hands for the Eucharistic Cup we are reaching out for the sacrament of ourselves, the fruit of the true Vine in the chalice answering to the fruit of the true Vine which we ourselves are. And as we have to become what we are on the paten – bread for the world, a source of nourishment for others – so we have to become what we are in the chalice – wine in other people's lives, that which loosens their tongue and gives them permission to say what is in their hearts. In the second and third centuries of the Christian era there were those who refused to use wine in the Eucharist, people known as Aquarians because the cup of their so-called celebration was a cup of water. Cyprian explains that they repudiate wine as intoxicating, and that is where they are false to the Scriptures, for the twenty-second psalm, the psalm of the mysteries, says precisely that the Lord's chalice *is* intoxicating. *Calix meus inebrians, quam praeclarus est*: 'My cup that inebriates, how wonderful it is!'[134] If we are to be consistent in our lives with what we practise in our sacraments we must be in some way intoxicating to people, a source for them of the joy which the Holy Spirit gives.

Yet we will almost certainly find that to be such a source of joy to others will mean suffering for us. The fruit of the true Vine which we drink in the Eucharist is the Blood of Christ, the blood of his sufferings and death. The fruit is pressed from the true Vine on the cross. If this plant is to flourish, and is truly to give that joy which rejoices gods and men, then it must be pruned savagely. A vine that grows wild and unpruned will soon cease to produce grapes of any size: it will be of use to no one. We can choose whether or not we will allow the Vinedresser to do his work 'for our good and the good of all the Church'.[135] We can resist his activity. We can have such a zest for our own wild life that we refuse to accept the limitations that will be necessary if we are to bear fruit for the life of the world. Normally, the way God will prune our vine will be through each other, for other people define by their needs the extent of the outward luxuriant growth that is possible for us. In the end the alternative to accepting the discipline of the Vinedresser is to be cut away from the Vine itself. Wood cut away from the vine is notoriously useless. 'Son of Man,' says Ezekiel to Jerusalem, 'how does the wood of the vine surpass any wood, the vine branch which is among the trees of the forest? Is wood taken from it to make anything? Do men ever take a peg from it to hang any vessel on?'[136] It is only as long as the branch continues to belong to the vine, as long as the sap of the Vine itself courses through it, that it is of any value to anyone.

Easter: the sixth Sunday[137]

'The grace of our Lord Jesus Christ, and the love of God and the
fellowship of the Holy Spirit be with you all': these are Paul's
closing words to his Corinthian converts. This fellowship of the
Holy Spirit, whose beginnings the Liturgy is about to celebrate,
stands as an unassailable given in the Church. The apostle can
simply take it as read when he writes to the Christians at Philippi:

> So if there is any comfort in Christ, if any consolation of love, if
> any fellowship of the Spirit, if any tender mercies and compas-
> sions, fulfil my joy, that you be of the same mind, having the
> same love, being of one accord, of one mind, doing nothing
> through faction or vainglory, but in lowliness of mind each count-
> ing others better than himself, not looking each of you to his own
> things but each of you also to the things of others.[138]

There then follows the famous hymn about how Christ, who was in
the form of God, humbled himself and was thereafter highly exalted.
This Christ Paul offers as a model for the Philippians: 'Let this
mind be in you which was also in Christ Jesus, who . . .'[139] Paul
simply assumes that there is such a thing as fellowship in the Spirit,
merely asking that this fellowship be expressed in the way people
live together, expressed, in fact, in a life-style which is that of Jesus
himself. The Letter to the Hebrews presupposes the same under-
girding fact when it describes Christians as those 'who were once
enlightened and tasted of the heavenly gift and were made partakers
of the Holy Spirit and tasted the good word of God and the powers
of the age to come.'[140] Grammatically it is entirely possible that
Paul's lapidary phrase, the fellowship of the Spirit, refers to that
fellowship between men and women that the Holy Spirit produces
in all his activity amongst Christians. In other words, it may be
another name for the Church, the Church seen under one of her

136

many aspects. The grace of our Lord Jesus Christ after all is a gift of Jesus; the love of God is the love which God shows towards us; so surely the fellowship of the Spirit lies in his effects among us. The Church, our Church, the Church that we are, is the work of the Spirit. Alternatively, the Pauline greeting could mean not so much that the Holy Spirit is the source of the activity which creates fellowship amongst Christians, but that he is what all Christians possess in common, in *koinonia* or fellowship. And why indeed may not both these shades of sense belong to the text and to the mind of Paul? The *koinonia* produced by the Holy Spirit was, and is, a result of *koinonia* in the Holy Spirit. The Church, our Church, the Church that we are is both formed by the Holy Spirit and shares out that Spirit as the one supreme Gift among so many gifts of the Father.

The Spirit in the Church is the gift of the Father. 'The love of God has been poured abroad in our hearts through the Holy Spirit which was given to us': so says Paul, in one of those common Jewish passives adopted in reverential circumlocution of the name of God. He is poured out as, in the Acts of the Apostles, the Holy Spirit was poured out on the day of Pentecost for the sake of those disciples in the Upper Room. Every time a person repents and is baptized what happened for the whole Church on that occasion happens for him as an individual. He enters into the communion of the Holy Spirit which the whole Church already enjoys, and through that communion in the Spirit he comes into communion with all his fellow Christians. The Church is the result of each man's communion with the Holy Spirit, though that communion may only be enjoyed provided that man does not close himself off from communion with all other Christians. The body does not produce the Spirit, although it is through the body that God pours out the wind and flame of Pentecost. As the physical body of Jesus was produced by the Holy Spirit from the Virgin Mary, so the church-body of Jesus is also produced by that same Spirit in whom all believers share in the experience of Pentecost. For St Luke, writing the Book of the Acts as the sequel to his gospel, no event seemed so much like the annunciation to Mary as did Pentecost. The Holy Spirit comes down on the Church as on Mary; the same power of the Most High is promised to Mary by the angel at the Incarnation and to the disciples by the ascending Jesus in the last of his resurrection appearances. Between Pentecost and the *Parousia* the Church will be in the Gift of the power of the Most High, the Church of the Holy Spirit.

In the New Testament the gift of the Spirit is expected to generate observable effects. Paul can tell the Thessalonians not to quench the Spirit; he can assume that the Galatians knew they had received the Spirit in the hearing of faith; he can make the experience of the varied gifts of the Spirit in the Roman Church a basis for this appeal for unity and holiness. In the Johannine Letters 'God has given us the Spirit'[141] appears to be a formula from the early Christian catechism. In the Book of the Acts it is the Spirit who, time and again, inspires the missionary activity of the Church. It is the Spirit who tells Philip to catch up with the coach of the Ethiopian who becomes his catechumen; it is the Spirit who, when Saul's persecution comes to an end, gives the comfort in which the Church throughout all Judaea and Galilee and Samaria can be built up and multiplied; it is the Spirit who tells Peter that three men are searching for him after his vision of the sheet let down from the sky, the start of the story of the conversion of Cornelius, the Gentile Pentecost. Similarly, it is the Spirit who tells the Church at Antioch; 'Separate for me Barnabas and Saul for the work to which I have called them.'[142] Finally, it is in the Spirit that John sees the visions of the Apocalypse, and the Spirit who speaks words of support or of judgement to the churches in that book. In other words, the early Church understood thoroughly and exhaustively that it was through the Spirit that her own inner life was founded, and through him that her work of spreading the gospel went forward.

From what the Spirit does and says to the Church at particular times and places, the move is made to an understanding of the abiding presence of the Spirit in the Church and in each believer. In the Letter to the Ephesians the Gentile Christians

> are no longer strangers and sojourners, but they are fellow-citizens with the saints, and of the household of God, being built upon the foundation of the apostles and prophets, Christ Jesus himself being the chief cornerstone, in whom every building, fitly framed together, grows into a holy temple in the Lord, in whom you also are built together into a habitation of God in the Spirit.[143]

The work of building is the work of the Spirit, but the building has the pattern and the plan of Jesus. The Spirit makes a single Temple, the flesh-body and the church-body of Jesus, just as he makes one new Man, the whole Christ. The Church is not simply some institution with its basic charter or constitution laid down by its founder at some point in past history. The Church is a reality in the Spirit. The agent for building up the Church is that Spirit who can only be spoken of in terms of wind and fire and water, in the most fluid of language. But the Spirit is not for that reason free-floating and unpredictable. He is the Spirit of that God who is faithful and true, the God whose activity is utterly self-consistent. The pattern for the Church is set in the historical life of Jesus: any activity which would run counter to that cannot be an activity proposed by the Spirit of God whom the Father poured out on the crucified Jesus and through him on all who are baptized into Jesus' death. There can be no radical cleavage between Spirit and institution. One would expect the work of the Spirit to produce institutions because it would naturally be a structuring activity. That is, one would expect the Spirit's work to be consistent with the creation of the body of flesh of Jesus of Nazareth: an incarnating activity, love seeking to express itself in forms, that love which is as much a technique as an emotion. There can be no ultimate incompatibility between Spirit and embodiment.

The Church which is the body of Christ is also the epiphany of the Holy Spirit. This is an epiphany in flesh, in the realm of the concrete and the particular, of what can be seen and heard. The Spirit is not of its nature hidden and inaccessible but, consistent with the action of God in the whole biblical tradition, he manifests himself in flesh and blood. He expresses himself in the Church by his transforming power, whether that power be of a quite spectacular sort, as in some of the charisms rediscovered by the Pentecostal Movement, or wholly unspectacular, as in such fruits of the Spirit as gentleness and faithfulness. Most typically, which does not mean in a time-worn way, the Spirit will epiphanize in the difference he makes to the whole life of the community, institutions and all; he shows himself in the increasing intensity of the one life that we may live with all men. It is on all flesh that the Spirit of God is poured out. All living things are, insofar as they are living, manifestations of the Spirit of God. The Spirit poured out in the end-times is meant to make them what they were made to be. He is to incorporate them into the world that was created in the Word of God. The Spirit and life cannot but belong together.

Ascension Day (or the seventh Sunday)[144]

It is not easy to get a true picture of Jesus. A late eighth-century Irish poem identified Jesus thus:

He is the First and the Last.
He is the second Adam and the brother of the first Adam.
He is the way and the truth and the life, and the mountain on which the city is set.
He is the true vine and the root of Jesse.
He is the consuming fire and the sacrificial Lamb.
He is the bread from heaven divided among the saints.
He is the strong lion of the tribe of Judah,
He is the flower of the field and the lily of the valley.
He is the sun of justice and the cornerstone, the giver of the light of the law and the great physician.

'He's just a man,' sings Mary Magdalene in *Jesus Christ Superstar*. 'He is our model and our rule', says Ignatius Loyola: *dechado y regla nuestra*.[145] Different generations of Christians see him in different ways, and they always see him partly, at least, in terms of the world where they themselves live. In early medieval society, where everyone had a place and knew it, where there was a system of mutual loyalty and protection in which each man took another as his *lord*, Jesus was primarily *our Lord*, the Lord of Christians. Nineteenth-century Englishmen of the dominant class pictured him in the image and likeness of an English public schoolboy. People on the suffering end of society saw him as weak and powerless, a failure, needing to be comforted and consoled. In the twentieth century he is Superstar, or he is a guerrilla leader. People must have needs and ideals, and they project these on to Jesus. Albert Schweitzer in his famous book on the quest of the historical Jesus shows without a doubt how true this is.

But we have to let our image of Jesus be changed and purified by the vantage-point of the New Testament. Even there, there are many different ways of understanding him, many different angles of approach to him, many different pictures of him. Nevertheless, the images we form of Jesus must always be referred to those scriptural attitudes in one way or another. No one biography could claim to be the last word on a person; yet no valid means of approach to Jesus can do without the picture offered by the gospels. The gospels are there to correct our defective images and they do so with great sureness of touch. In the gospels, for example, Jesus is called *Lord*; but what a Greek of the first century meant by that is not at all what a feudal German meant by it in the eleventh. And neither Greek nor German could have coped with a lord who donned an apron and waited at table. The English gentlemanly Jesus does not fit easily with the rough-tongued, blasting Jesus of Matthew's gospel. The loving heart of Jesus, as that is revealed to us in the Fourth Gospel, seems a far cry from the heart of Jesus in modern devotion. Superstar would surely not have refused to put on a show in the Temple courtyard. The guerrilla leader would not have taken the decision Jesus took at the Last Supper: he would have let his followers put their swords to the use for which they had been made and bought. All our ideas of Jesus must be purified by the gospel account. Unless we enter into communion with Jesus in his inspired word, indeed, our prayer at communion may be the addressing of a graven image.

To see Jesus you have to turn. John the Elder says in the Book of the Apocalypse, 'I turned to see the voice which spoke with me'.[146] In order to see he turns or converts. John had heard the voice, and believed accordingly: he had the faith that comes from hearing. But it was a faith that sought understanding, and so he turned to see. It helps to know where to turn. John turned and looked to see the voice which spoke to him in the candlestick vision of the Book of Zechariah. He was right to do so, because Jesus is there. Later he looks to other books of the Bible – there is scarcely a canonical writing to which he does not allude somewhere in the Apocalypse – and in them all he finds Jesus. John began that meditative exploration of Scripture memories in which the Church has been engaged ever since in her love affair with Jesus, approaching it from so many different angles. In his turning he sees Jesus of Nazareth, the Jesus who died and, look! he is alive for evermore. He sees the Jesus who walks in glory in the midst of the lampstands, clothed with gold, his eyes like a flame of fire and his feet like burnished bronze, but still the son of man, the same person whom the disciples in Galilee had known and followed. The Christ of our faith is none other than the Jesus of history, the Jesus who had called fishermen and tax-collectors, who had troubled them and judged them, loved them and consoled them on their travels. It is still the same Jesus judging and consoling his Church. John sees the ascended Jesus who is now the Lord and the Christ, the Lion of Judah who has conquered. But when he looks again he sees instead a lamb, its throat cut open. A *Lamb*, that is, a man who was butchered: he it is who is Lord. In our celebration of Easter and Ascensiontide, in all our Paschal joy and exultation, in all the new triumphalism which has shifted from the Church to Jesus we can never forget this truth. It is the Lamb who is the Lion of Judah. The risen and ascended Conqueror is the Lamb with the marks of slaughter still upon him. The central image of Christianity remains the crucified Lord Jesus.

When we celebrate the Ascension we are not so much remembering the last time that Jesus took leave of his disciples, perhaps in some rather spectacular way. Rather, we are trying to realize and to celebrate the way Jesus now is, just as John attempts to realize it for us in the picture he offers us. Fra Angelico, in his paintings of the crucifixion, shows us, it has been said, no longer an event of the remote past reconstituted in the painter's imagination, but the image of a sacrifice represented anew each day in Christian worship. Similarly, John's word-painting aims not to represent but to show forth and to celebrate.

The Jesus of John's vision has the keys of Death and Hades, just as the Jesus of Matthew's gospel has been given all authority in heaven and on earth. God has given a resounding 'Yes' to Jesus, to the Jesus who was such an outgoing person that he emptied himself, he went all out for us, even to the death of the cross. God has given a firm 'Amen' to the Jesus who for ever shows the signs that he is such a person, the signs that came over him once and for all when he was nailed to the cross and pierced by the lance, the signs that continue in the open side and the nail-marks of the resurrection appearances. In the gospels, as in the vision of John, it is by this and by this alone that Jesus can be recognized for who he is. The 'Yes' God gave to Jesus in raising him from the grave resounds in the Ascension. Jesus has received, we say, 'all authority'. His life, focussed and summarised in his death, is now authoritative for all

142

times and all places. It sets the pattern and forms the God-given model for the lives of people at all times and in all places. That pattern of living, and only that, has any final value as a way of being man.

But all this is only visible to the eyes of faith. Jesus is taken up as his apostles, those who believe in him, look on. God made their faith *oculata*, as St Thomas would say: he gave eyes to their believing. The fact that Jesus has gone up in the world, receiving as his own all authority, is not the kind of fact that is open to casual observation. It is only clear to those who believe in him. Or rather, believing in him means seeing, in some way or another such as with the eyes of John in the Apocalypse, that God has given him his resounding 'Yes' and 'Amen'. Faith means living as people who do see that. It involves translating that vision into practice, whether the practice of words in talking about the gospel, or the practice of deeds, in the imitation of the crucified Jesus from whom God will never withdraw his assent.

Vigil of Pentecost

'Look,' says Jesus, 'I am sending forth the promise of my Father upon you. But you stay here in the city until you are clothed with power from on high.'[147] And then, perhaps scarcely knowing what they are waiting or praying for, the Church comes together in prayer. That Upper Room is where we are expected to see them, that room of the Last Supper and the resurrection coming of Jesus, the place where eventually the Holy Spirit would come and fill all the house where they were sitting. It is the place of the Church, the room of the mysteries. It is St Catherine's image for prayer, her equivalent and translocation of the Carmelite image of the desert, or the mountain. It is also St Thomas' source for religious life which he says 'originates in the life of the disciples after the resurrection'.[148]

In that Upper Room which is the place of the Eucharist and of the Spirit the disciples prayed in common. They prayed unanimously, in a prayer of a single accord. The word, which is a favourite one throughout the Acts of the Apostles suggests that 'one heart and one soul' apparent in the Jerusalem church soon after the Holy Spirit came upon them in power at Pentecost, and embodied in their having all things in common. Being of one accord is not the least striking feature of an apostolic community. It is this sense of common being and common praying that we have been slowly and laboriously trying to recapture over the last few years in the Church. Certainly there is a place for solitary prayer. It is not a matter of taste but of precept that we should pray in solitude, shutting our door on others to pray to the Father in secret. If we never pray in that secrecy and solitude, by ourselves, then the quality of our prayer together will be poor indeed. But equally, it is a matter not of taste but of command and example from the apostolic church that we pray together. Such prayer together is not meant to be the prayer of a lot of people each at that moment in their own invisible little room. Upper Room prayer, the prayer of a truly apostolic church, means the prayer of persons who are conscious of the others present and of the great company of all faithful people who surround us. It is the prayer of a community, not that of a crowd. In all this we cannot simply assume that because we come into one place to pray we are straightaway praying in common, apostolically, with one heart and soul. Being under the same roof is not enough. Being with other people we know well, even our own religious family, is not enough. For, in that Upper Room, among the group were the brethren of Jesus, his own immediate family. Yet we know that, not long before, those brothers of his had not formed part of his following. Now they were present not as his kith and kin, for that gave them no claim on the Christian fellowship, but as his disciples.

We are to pray then, as a congregation, that is, a gathered flock, and not as a hundred lost sheep who happen to have strayed simultaneously into the same building. The church in which we pray, the Upper Room, is not limited, however, by the walls of the building. It holds all the people of God, living and departed. And it is here that Mary the mother of Jesus has her place. All the good things for which we are told to pray can be summarized, as Luke summarizes them, in the plea for the Holy Spirit, *the* Gift of God. At the heart of the praying church, as it prays now for a new Pentecost, is Mary the mother of Jesus. She stands amongst us as the Church's praying centre, the witness to the centrality of prayer in the life of the people of God. We do not necessarily and always have to look towards Mary, but we do have to look with her to the Father, through the Son, in the Holy Spirit. Prayer is Marian if it is prayer with her, prayer that prays within the communion of saints that she brings into focus. In the Church we are gathered with her and with her look to where Jesus is, seated at the right hand of God. With her we pray through Jesus to the Father. This is the pattern we find in the Eucharist where we pray directly and immediately through, with and in Jesus to his God and Father and ours and where 'in union with the whole Church we honour Mary, the ever-virgin mother of Jesus Christ, our Lord and God.'[149] The image of Mary praying before Pentecost is literally the ultimate image of Mary given us in the New Testament. The pentecostal praying for all those good things summed up in the Spirit himself as Gift is what we are about each year between Ascension and Pentecost. This period of time concentrates one constant quality of Christian living, prayer for the coming of the Spirit, and in particular this is what we do at the Vigil of Pentecost.

145

At today's Vigil the Church gives us to read the gospel about Jesus calling people to come to him and drink. It is, we are told, the last day, the great day of the feast. The Jewish feast is not named, for the Liturgy invites us to hear these words in the new context of the feast of Easter, the fifty days of the Paschal celebration of Christians. Pentecost is the last and great day of that feast. It is the last in the sense of the final day, but it is also the ultimate or eschatological day when we anticipate the pouring out of the Holy Spirit upon all flesh at the end of time. It is the great day, the crown of Easter as the Liturgy puts it, as well as its close. As Peter takes up Joel's prophecy in his Pentecost sermon it is a day of epiphany, when Easter comes out and goes public. It is the day when Easter breaks out from behind the closed doors, where the disciples are hiding in their fear, and takes to the streets. And as we hear the gospel read to us on this Vigil we are asked to see Jesus amongst us, standing up and shouting out his invitation, now, on this particular Pentecost Eve, at the beginning of the last day, the great day, the crown and close of Easter.

' "He who believes on me, [Jesus says to us] out of his heart shall flow rivers of living water." This he spoke of the Spirit which those who believed in him were to receive; for the Spirit was not yet, because Jesus was not yet glorified'.[150] The Spirit was not yet; it was not yet Spirit, as we might say, 'It was not yet Spring.' We feel that we must explain this odd text and even explain it away, glossing it and hedging it with footnotes, as so many Christians have done through history. Can it really be that the Spirit was not yet? After all, according to the Old Testament the Spirit of God breathed over the face of the deep in the beginning. The Spirit of God was in Joseph to interpret the dreams of Pharoah. The Lord filled Bezalel the son of Uri 'with the Spirit of God, in wisdom and in understanding and in knowledge and in all manner of workmanship, to devise cunning works, to work in gold and in silver and in brass, and in the cutting of stones for setting and in the carving of wood, for work in every craft'.[151] Joshua the son of Nun was filled with the Spirit of wisdom. 'The Spirit of the Lord clothed himself with Gideon'[152] wrapping him right round him. The Spirit came mightily upon Samson, as upon Othniel and upon Jephthah, and Samson 'tore a young lion in pieces as easily as he would have done a young goat; and he had nothing in his hand'.[153] The Spirit of the Lord came mightily upon him, and the ropes which the Philistines had put on his arms 'became as flax that was burnt with fire, and his bands

146

were melted from off his hands'.[154] The Spirit of the Lord came down upon Balaam and he prophesied. 'The Lord came down in the cloud . . . and took of the Spirit that was upon Moses, and put it upon the seventy elders, and they prophesied.'[155] Micah was 'filled with the Spirit of the Lord and with judgement and with might, to declare to Jacob his transgression and to Israel his sin.'[156] The Spirit of the Lord turned Saul into another man, a new person. When Samuel took the horn of oil and anointed David in the midst of his brethren 'the Spirit of the Lord leapt upon him,'[157] as the Septuagint puts it. The Spirit of God came upon Azariah, the son of Oded, and inspired him to go out and meet King Asa and encourage him to be strong enough to destroy the idols in Judah and Benjamin and to renew the altar of the Lord. The wise man in the Wisdom says: 'The Spirit of the Lord has filled the whole earth, and his immortal Spirit is in all things.'[158] But the Spirit was not yet. To anyone familiar with the story of God's dealing with Israel, it was hard to credit that John, who was so much at home in his Old Testament, could ever have written that 'as yet there was no Spirit'. No wonder that people tried to amend his text.

When Jesus was in the prime of his age, on this last and great day of the feast when he invited those who believed in him to come and drink, there was as yet no Spirit. But John the Baptist had been filled with the Spirit from his mother's womb. Elizabeth had been filled with the Holy Spirit, and in that Spirit she had blessed Mary and her unborn child. Zechariah had been filled with the Holy Spirit in his prophesying over the infant Baptist. The Holy Spirit was upon old Simeon; and it had been revealed to him by the Holy Spirit that he should not see death before he had seen the Lord's Anointed. He came in the Spirit into the Temple when Joseph and Mary brought in the child Jesus. The Holy Spirit came down upon Mary, and the power of the Most High overshadowed her and she was found to be with child of the Holy Spirit. When Jesus grew up and was baptized in the Jordan the Spirit came down upon him. The Spirit led him into the desert, and full of the Spirit he returned into Galilee. He rejoiced in the Spirit at the success of the mission of the seventy-two disciples. But 'as yet there was no Spirit'.

Now St John knew his Old Testament, and he knew about the Spirit in Jesus. Nevertheless, he could write plainly and bluntly that the Spirit was not yet because Jesus was not yet glorified. In comparison with what was yet to be, with the pouring out of the Spirit

147

through the glorified body of Jesus in the pentecostal experience of the Spirit in the Church, he could say that all previous experience of the Spirit was as nothing. In comparison with what was yet to be, the summer, the unimaginable zero summer, there had been no Spirit. 'Midwinter spring is its own season . . . not in time's covenant.'[159] We too are invited by the Church's Liturgy to prepare for a coming of the Holy Spirit in comparison with which it will seem that as yet in our lives there was no Holy Spirit. We too, like the Israel of old, are far from strangers to the Spirit. We have entered into the inheritance of that Israel, the Spirit-filled people of God. We have been given the Holy Spirit at our baptism, and at our confirmation we received him for witness and mission in the sacrament, which as its Liturgy says, 'perpetuates pentecostal grace in the church'. The Spirit has been manifested in our particular charisms, in our gifts and talents. For some of us it has always been gentle, silent: the still waters of the Spirit running deep. We can represent the Spirit of Pentecost in our lives by smooth mapping, the long and steady walk with God, marked with his renewal through the sacraments which bring us forgiveness and healing. For others of us, it seemed as though his flow had been blocked and then released quite suddenly and overwhelmingly in what we may want to call a second conversion or perhaps even, though unwisely, 'the baptism of the Holy Spirit'. We may be less aware of the steady growth and manifestation of the Spirit than of the breaks he has produced, the discontinuity, the qualitative change, the 'catastrophe' in the mathematical sense of that word. A walk with God certainly; but for some of us it was as though while walking with him we suddenly stepped off the top of a cliff. The next step in such a case is not just one of a series with its predecessors! But even those of us whose experience of the Holy Spirit has been one of his sudden and mighty coming are invited now, at today's Vigil, to something more. Our experience of the Lord goes from beginning to beginning. Just as Mary, on whom the Holy Spirit had come at the Annunciation, could still pray for the coming of Power from on high so we who pray with Mary before Pentecost for the Spirit's coming can receive him in such a way that we can say, 'In comparison with this, there was not yet Spirit.'

Perhaps he will come to us as though it were flood-gates suddenly breaking. Perhaps he will come and manifest himself in a quieter faith and a steadier confidence. But in either case we are asked not to make a stand on what we have already received, sacramentally or charismatically. We must not sink back content with what God has given us but ask for more for, in comparison with the best wine which he keeps till the end, we have no wine as yet. We show our gratitude to God for the gifts he has given us precisely by asking for more. God can give us so much more than he has given us as yet that everything we have received until now can seem, in comparison, as though it had never been.

Pentecost

As St Luke tells the story of the crucifixion and death of Jesus, the first words Jesus says are 'Father, forgive!'[160] For Luke, this prayer of Jesus, that God should forgive everything and everyone, is a summary of the whole gospel. It is prayer immediately answered. When Jesus died, we are told, all the crowds that came together to this sight, when they beheld the things that were done, returned beating their breasts, that is, repenting; and such repentance was of itself forgiveness. The gift of repentance, of a broken and contrite heart, is the reflection in us of God's free forgiving. When at this sight, or spectacle, or showing, of God's love we repent and turn, that is the effect in us of God's forgiveness of the world, the prayer of Jesus availing in us, general absolution.

'General absolution' is the name we give to a particular way of celebrating the sacrament of repentance, that sacrament which is inadequately described as 'confession' because it can be celebrated quite properly without any particular confession of specific sins, as so many people have discovered in recent years to their great joy. It might seem that general absolution is cheap absolution. God's forgiveness is indeed entirely free but it is not for that reason cheap. The price to be paid for forgiveness is the life of Jesus poured out in love for God and for us. On our side, the price to be paid is not necessarily the embarrassment of confessing particular sins, laying ourselves open to having a strip torn off us. Forgiveness can be costly without that, for its cost is repentance. Without repentance there can be no absolution, not because God has for some reason or other decided it that way but because, in the nature of things, two persons cannot be reconciled unless both want it. If I hurt another person he can go on forgiving and forgiving me, but unless I want to be friends again we are not friends. So it is in the sacrament of reconciliation with God. The priest or the bishop may pronounce absolution over me; but unless I want to be reconciled

150

with God it does me no good. Indeed, it may do me harm by making me *blasé*. Wthout real repentance the sacrament is at best without effect. Sacraments do not have an automatic effect in our lives, working on us as though they were food or medicine. The effects they have on us depend on the attitude of heart and mind we bring to them. And so the effect of the sacrament of penance in our lives depends on what we expect from it in our lives.

What can we expect? The narratives of Scripture spell out for us the consequences of Jesus' prayer that God should forgive, and hence they enabie us to answer that question. One such story is that of the coming of the risen Jesus to his disciples on the evening of Easter Day, in the Upper Room when the doors were shut. It is a story which bridges the gap between the death of Jesus and his risen presence. The forgiving Jesus of Easter and Pentecost is recognizably the forgiving Jesus of the cross. In this 'Johannine Pentecost' story we are given an image of what is meant to happen in and through the sacrament of penance. The restored rite of celebrating that sacrament, by its words and gestures, is intended to make that gospel story happen in our lives. The form of absolution first tells the story of what God has done: 'God, the Father of mercies, by the death and resurrection of his Son has reconciled the world to himself and sent the Holy Spirit among us for the forgiveness of sins.'[161] Then, having rehearsed what God has accomplished, the rite prays that this may be actual for us now: 'Through the ministry of the Church may God give you pardon and peace.' Pardon: the return of Jesus is itself such pardon, the Lord coming and standing amongst them; and peace: the first words, the signature tune, of the Easter Jesus. And not only the words but also the gestures of the rite re-create the story. The gesture of laying on of hands or of stretching out of hands is the equivalent of Jesus breathing the Holy Spirit on the disciples, for it depicts the gesture of that Jesus who stands at the right hand of God with his own hands stretched out in blessing on the world. This hand movement is the gesture used in all sacraments where the primary gift is the Holy Spirit. It is the particular gesture of confirmation, when the Holy Spirit is given us for mission, so that we may be witnesses of Jesus in our world. It is the gesture of ordination, when the Spirit is given for special service in the Christian community. It is the gesture in the anointing of the sick, when the Spirit is given for healing, for making men whole. Above all, it is the gesture in the sacrament of repentance, when the Holy Spirit is given as forgiveness. As Jerome said so long

151

ago, 'The priest lays his hand on the penitent to invoke the return of the Holy Spirit.'[162] The gift we are given in this sacrament is the Spirit himself.

The Holy Spirit is himself the forgiveness of sins, according to a prayer of the Liturgy around Pentecost. So absolution cannot be primarily a statement from the priest saying that we are now cleared and acquitted because we have paid our debt to God and to the society of the Church and therefore can enjoy the Eucharist again. Fundamentally absolution must be, rather, this new sending of the Holy Spirit, a renewing of our baptism and our confirmation, the Holy Spirit coming to make us new men and women again. What we should want when we come to the sacrament (whether we celebrate it at a general absolution, or with shared preparation and thanksgiving, or altogether one-to-one) is this gift of the recreating Holy Spirit. If we do not expect as much as that from this sacrament it is unlikely that we will get as much as that. And then the sacrament will have been robbed of a good deal of its power.

In the Pentecost of the Third Gospel St Luke found that he could best describe the Holy Spirit as a rushing mighty wind, and as flames of fire. It is thoroughly understandable that, if the Spirit is himself the forgiveness of sins, he should be spoken of in terms of fire. So often our image of forgiveness is watery. We think of the blotting out of sins, or the wiping clean of the slate. This picture of the total disappearance of anything God might have against us is in its own way a valid and perhaps at times a necessary one. Yet surely the image of forgiveness as fire is more significant. If sin is blotted out, its record erased, its slate wiped clean, it is only too likely that the writing tablet will be written on again. The house swept and garnished is a standing invitation to a squat by seven spirits more wicked than the one we first got rid of. Possibly we should think more of sin as being burned up in the pentecostal fires of the Holy Spirit. The new thing that comes into our lives deals with what is old and dead, and so makes us new people.

What would it be like to be new men and women in Jesus through his Holy Spirit? The New Testament is full of the answer to this. It talks about a whole new relationship with God in which 'his commandments are not burdensome',[163] not a heavy weight to bear. Living the Christian life should be no longer the dull slog we can so easily find it to be, in our desperate attempts to keep on the straight and narrow. We can so easily make Christianity pre-Christian, and curiously enough, this is nowhere more true than with this business of repentance. We have to repent even about repentance. We have to undergo a change of heart and mind on that subject too. Contrast, for instance, Jonah with Jesus. Jonah went a day's journey into the city of Nineveh, crying, 'Yet forty days, and Nineveh shall be destroyed.'[164] And the people of Nineveh believed God and turned from their evil way. Jesus came into Galilee preaching the good news of God and saying, 'The time is fulfilled and the kingdom of God is on top of you; repent and believe in the good news.'[165] These two stories are not variants on a theme: there is a world of difference between them. Why should you change your attitude to life and the way you live? Because yet forty days and Nineveh shall be overthrown? Or because the time is fulfilled and the Kingdom of God is right at the door? Do we repent because of the threat to us if we don't, or because of the promise held out to us if we do? Neither of those motives is adequate to the Christian reality of repentance. Long before Christianity is any kind of ethical requirement, before it is a matter of morals and behaviour, it is gospel or good news about what is there beyond ourselves. It is the good news of something supremely unjust and quite amoral, the answered prayer of Jesus: 'Father, forgive them, for they know not what they do.' It is the good news of God dealing with this world on the basis of acceptance and forgiveness and thus becoming King. Change your outlook to embrace that, says Jesus. Stop thinking and acting as though God and yourself are related chiefly as lawgiver and subject. Stop thinking that the relationship between God and man is primarily a matter of justice in some ordinary sense of that word. Believe the altogether extraordinary and unlooked for and wellnigh unbelievable news that God has freely chosen to be God in a quite different way to this world, to be God as he who forgives and loves and accepts.

To accept this new basis for living with God and other people is to be freed for a genuine change of heart and mind. This is what frees us from presumption, because we can do nothing to win the love of God. That love is ours already as a free gift from the free God. This is what frees us, too, from despair, because our weakness and failures and falling back cannot separate us from the love of God. That love is always there if we will have it so, wanting it from our heart of hearts, reaching out for it in no matter how formless a way and taking it, believing that this is the God we now have in Jesus. To live in the love of God is to begin the process of the long

153

slow maturing of the Christian character which is what distinctively Christian morality is all about, the ripening of the harvest of the Spirit which is given us.

Trinity Sunday

The Trinity, we assume, is a great problem for our minds. On Trinity Sunday the preacher is expected to do something towards elucidating this conundrum, although from past experience he will probably only make the darkness doubly dark. We expect to hear something of what Luther called the mathematics of the Godhead, about what is at once three and one, one and three. We suppose that we must try again to make sense of strange connections of persons and nature, of begettings and proceedings, strange words and stranger ideas, picked up from Catechisms, perhaps, or from the so-called Athanasian Creed, telling of the three who are distinct from each other and yet are altogether one. In the Dominican tradition Trinity Sunday is the day when the brightest theologian in the house, the Regent of Studies, the *primus doctor*, preaches the sermon at the liturgy of the brethren. How quickly that can lead to talk about talk, to using words to say what are the appropriate words to use about the Blessed Trinity. For today's feast is a feast of orthodoxy, a celebration of the correct ways of talking about the God who can scarcely be talked about. Here at least lie the origins of the feast in the Calendar, for St Thomas Becket introduced it at a time when theology in England was vigorously alive, when people loved to talk about the central concerns of the faith and about none more than the Trinity, and when the theology of the triune God was again attracting the attention of brilliant minds after lying dormant for centuries. The feast of the Trinity was a feast for the theologians in the narrow sense, an occasion for the bright boys to let go.

It would be a pity to underplay that by underestimating the importance of right belief. What a man believes is not incidental to how a man lives, granted always that it is a question of what a man really and truly believes and not purely and simply of what he is prepared to say that he believes. How you live depends in fact on what you really believe, on what you are prepared to put your trust in, and to stake yourself on. Perhaps it is all to the good that once in a while we should celebrate not, as in the usual Christian tradition, some concrete historical event which has changed our lives but simply the One who is the source of those events. Gently contemplating him in whom we put our faith we can let the words we utter about the Three-in-One and One-in-Three bemuse and bewitch us. We can deliberately let ourselves get lost, once in a while, in the paradoxes of the language of orthodoxy, for going beyond reason is part of the significance of *metanoia*, repentance.

Christianity is an historical religion through and through. It is concerned with the events God has brought about for our well-being, as St Thomas would say, to make us happy. For us and for our happiness the Word of God became a man of flesh and blood, altogether one of us. That is what we celebrated at Christmas and on the Epiphany. For our sakes too, the Word of God made flesh was crucified, suffered death and was buried in the time of Pontius Pilate. That is what we commemorate in Holy Week. Then for our well-being the Word who had become man and who had been killed was raised again in the Holy Spirit from amongst the dead. We celebrate that in the fifty days of Easter. And then, so that we might be fully happy, the Father sent the Spirit through the Son. That is what we concern ourselves with at Pentecost. But when we keep Trinity Sunday it seems that we are not really being encouraged to remember anything in this way at all. You can only remember what is, in one sense at least, in the past. Today we concern ourselves instead with what happens in time out of time. We look to how *God* happens, to how God is in himself. It is true that we could never know how God is in himself if we knew nothing of what he had done, but knowing that we do know God in himself. There is nothing extraordinary about that condition of knowing God. After all, we only know what one of our fellow men is like by looking at what he or she does. Through this characteristic behaviour of God we rejoice to know that he is good and loving and true. Deeper still, in how God is God, we delight in the mystery of his being Father, Son and Holy Spirit.

A mystery, we are told, is beyond reason. That suggests that the more we reason the closer we approach it, although it always lies on the further side. But that is not the meaning of 'mystery' in this context. Of course we have to try and understand as thoroughly as possible what it is we believe. We have a duty laid on us to love

God with all our mind, as well as with all our heart and soul and strength. But while problems are there to be solved by brain-power, mysteries are to be lived with, lived from and lived out. Sometimes in colloquial English we use the word 'mystery' when we would do better to talk of 'problem'. The point of a mystery movie is that the mystery gets cleared up; before a tale of mystery and adventure ends the mystery is unravelled and we go off to bed knowing the answer. The Trinity, on the other hand, is a mystery which cannot be solved for there is no problem about it. It is too flat a view of reality which assumes that all we encounter in life are problems to be solved. People, for instance, may have problems yet people are not problems. Every human being is a mystery in his or her own right, and woe betide us if we treat other people or ourselves as jumbles to be sorted out. We have always to live with one another as people beyond our control and manipulation. And equally, we have always to live with ourselves as the mystery which we are. We cannot put a person into words with no remainder left over. Everything we say about people always leaves the mystery of each person intact. As for each human being, so for the origin and ground of all things, for God. That off-putting language about 'one and three, persons and natures' is there to remind us that we must not attempt to solve the Trinity as though God were a problem. We are being told, in the classical formulae of Christian faith, that we have to say apparently contradictory things about God if we are to get anywhere near the truth.

The mystery which God is, that he has shown us in what we call the history of salvation. At the burning bush Moses asks God to tell him his name. The most likely translation of God's speech is, 'I will be whom I will be.'[166] Although God lets Moses see that he is the God of the fathers he insists that it is less important to know what he has been and is than to know that this is less significant than what he will be. The Old Testament, correspondingly, is full of this sense: it is not yet clear what God's name will be. Only in the New Testament do we get intimations that the mystery has been revealed. That is because the New Testament writings share the conviction that God has spoken a definitive word to us, that this Word has been made flesh and dwelt among us in the decisive act in the drama of God's dealings with men. Indeed, people were so staggered by what happened in Jesus of Nazareth that they had to rethink their whole idea of what it was for God to be God. In Jesus they heard one who spoke as though he had the authority of

God himself. They met one whose authority was vindicated when God raised him from the dead. And yet they experienced in him someone conscious of standing before the God of Israel and addressing him as 'Abba, Father'. And when the presence of that man ceased, at least in the form they had known, they were conscious of another presence with them. This presence was not Jesus, for it told them about Jesus, neither was it the God whom Jesus called Father, for they continued to pray 'Father'. This other presence which they called the Spirit seemed to speak in their hearts and consciences with authority as absolute as that of the Father and of Jesus yet which ·pointed them both to Jesus and to the Father. They were conscious, therefore, of three centres of power: power within them, the Spirit, power beside them, Jesus; power above them, the Father. It took centuries to work out the relationship of these three from that basis of experience. The Church worked it out in a language which solved nothing but forbade the taking of short cuts. No aspect of the threefold experience might be discounted; every aspect pointed in some way to a single source.

Behind the story of the Lord God of Israel, and Jesus his Son and his Holy Spirit there is a stillness and a single moment. *How* it is single will perhaps remain unclarified until the end. As the prophet Zechariah said, 'On that day the Lord will be one and his name one.'[167] That may well be our best approach: to live with the experience we are baptized into sharing, praying to the Father, with the Son, in the Holy Spirit, and leaving it to the threefold Lord to show us in the future how his name is one. As the Athanasian Creed has it: 'Now the Catholic faith is this – that we worship one God in Trinity and Trinity in Unity.'

Notes

1 This text is based on Isaiah 63:16–17, 64:1, 36–8, for the Mass of the First Sunday of Advent in the second year of the triennial cycle of the Roman Lectionary (Rome, 1970).
2 Isaiah 63:17
3 The *Rorate Caeli*, which takes its name from Isaiah 45:8, is essentially a Christian meditation on Isaiah 64. See Dom Prosper Guéranger, *The Liturgical Year* (English Translation, Dublin 1870), pp. 155–6.
4 Isaiah 64:6
5 Mark 13:33 and parallels.
6 All three gospels given for the Mass of the Second Sunday of Advent deal with St John the Baptist: Matthew 3:1–12; Mark 1:1–8; Luke 3:1–6.
7 From the *Sanctus* of the Roman Rite.
8 Apocalypse 1:8
9 John 1:29, 36
10 John 1:8
11 John 5:35
12 Matthew 11:14
13 Matthew 11:9
14 Matthew 11:11
15 This text starts out from Zephaniah 3:14–18, the First Reading for the Mass of the Third Sunday of Advent, in the third year of the Lectionary cycle.
16 Zephaniah 3:14–15
17 Luke 1:45
18 Luke 1:38
19 *The Roman Martyrology*, sub loc.
20 *Conditor alme siderum*, the Advent Vespers hymn of the *Antiphonale Romanum*.
21 Exodus 3:13–14
22 Habakkuk 2:2
23 Apocalypse 1:19
24 1 John 4:19
25 Exodus 3:3
26 Proper Preface of the Second Eucharistic Prayer in the Roman Rite.
27 Matthew 1:1
28 Isaiah 11:1

29 John Donne, *Holy Sonnets, Divine Meditations*, 14
30 The Starets Silouan of Athos. See Archimandrite Sofrony, *The Undistorted Image* (Faith Press, London 1958), p. 200.
31 Ephesians 6:12
32 Zechariah 3:8 (Vulgate)
33 Zechariah 6:12 (Vulgate)
34 Luke 1:78–9
35 Malachi 4:2
36 Fourth Eucharistic Prayer in the Roman Rite.
37 This text from the Passover Haggadah may be found in Chaim Raphael, *A Feast of History* (Weidenfeld & Nicholson, London 1972), p. 43 (214)
38 Psalm 136:25.
39 The writings of Abbot Rupert of Deutz, near Cologne (c. 1070–1129), may be found in volumes 117–20 in J. P. Migne, *Patrologia Latina*, (221 vols, Paris 1844–64).
40 This text is based on Luke 2:41–52, the Gospel for the Feast of the Holy Family, in the third year of the Lectionary cycle.
41 2 Chronicles 36:23
42 Luke 2:42
43 Luke 2:48
44 Matthew 23:9
45 Tertullian, *De Oratione* II, *Patrologia Latina* I, 1153B.
46 Luke 2:48
47 Luke 2:11
48 Psalm 103:3
49 Second Vatican Council, *Decree on the Missionary Activity of the Church (Ad Gentes)*, 2
50 Clement of Alexandria, *Paedagogos* I, 6. *Patrologia Graeca* 8, 282C.
51 Ibid., 40
52 St Augustine, *Retractiones* 12, 3, *Patrologia Latina*, 32, 603
53 Matthew 6:1–6, 16–18
54 James 2:18
55 Leo the Great, *De Quadragesima Sermo XI*, 6. *Patrologia Latina*, 54, 305B
56 Robert Herrick, 'To Keep a True Lent', *Noble Numbers*, p. 228
57 Compare the Readings for the First Sunday of Lent in the first year of the Lectionary cycle, Genesis 2:7–9; 3:1–7; Romans 5:12–19 and Matthew 4:1–11.
58 John Donne, *Eighty Sermons* (1640), Sermon 2
59 John 19:5
60 E. Rickert (ed.), *Ancient English Christmas Carols* (London 1910), pp. 163–4
61 Genesis 3:8
62 Augustine, *Soliloquies* 2, 1, *Patrologia Latina* 32, 885B
63 All three First Readings for the second Sunday of Lent deal with the figure of Abraham, Genesis 12:1–4; 22:1–2, 9a, 10–13, 15–18; 15:5–12; 17–18.
64 Genesis 11:2,4
65 The prayer *Suscipe quaesumus Domine* of the Roman Canon

66 Genesis 11:31–2
67 Genesis 12:1
68 Apocalypse 18:4
69 Hebrews 11:8
70 Genesis 13:16
71 Genesis 16:12
72 Genesis 22:2
73 The Gospel of the Samaritan Woman John 4:5–42 is read on the Third Sunday of Lent in the first year of the Lectionary cycle.
74 John 4:7
75 John 19:28
76 John 19:30
77 Julian of Norwich, *Revelations of Divine Love*, Ch. 31
78 John 19:29
79 Matthew 25:35
80 St Benedict, *Rule*, Ch. 58
81 Psalm 42:1
82 Placid Conway OP, *St Thomas Aquinas* (Longmans Green, London 1911). p. 88
83 Julian of Norwich, Ibid., Ch. 31
84 The Liturgy on this feast contemplates the figure of David in 1 Samuel 16:1, 6–7, 10–13, the First Reading for the fourth Sunday of Lent in the first year of the Lectionary cycle.
85 Robert Frost, from 'Build Soil', *A Further Range* (H. Holt and Co., New York 1936, and J. Cape, London 1937).
86 Second Vatican Council, *Dogmatic Constitution on the Church (Lumen Gentium)*, 1
87 Aboth Rabbi Nathan, vers. I, XXVIII, 439, see C. G. Montefiore and H. Loewe, *A Rabbinic Anthology*, (New York 1974), p. 530.
88 The Gospel of the Raising of Lazarus John 11:1–45 is read on the Fifth Sunday of Lent in the first year of the Lectionary cycle.
89 Psalm 48:2
90 John 11:25–6
91 Psalm 11:9 (Vulgate)
92 John 11:44
93 John 10:9
94 Mark 8:29 and parallels
95 Ignatius of Antioch, *To the Philadelphians*, 9
96 Apocalypse 3:8
97 Matthew 25:6
98 Matthew 23:37–8 and Lucan parallel
99 *Odes of Solomon*, 17, (Oxford University Press, Oxford 1973)
100 Psalm 22:1
101 Psalm 22:8
102 Psalm 88:8, 18
103 John 5:7
104 1 John 3:8
105 Luke 23:46
106 John 19:30

107 Luke 23:46
108 Psalm 30:6 (Vulgate)
109 John 12:25
110 W. B. Yeats, from his poem 'The Friends that Have It I Do Wrong'
111 John 20:22
112 Luke 24:39–40
113 Matthew 27:40
114 John Donne, 'The Cross'
115 Philippians 2:7
116 This text is based on John 20:19–31, the Gospel for the Second Sunday of Eastertide.
117 Luke 24:39
118 John 20:27
119 This meditation starts out from Luke 24:13–35, the Gospel of the Third Sunday of Eastertide in the first year of the Lectionary cycle.
120 John 21:12
121 All the Gospel texts for the Mass of the Fourth Sunday of Eastertide concern themselves with Jesus as the Good Shepherd. John 10:1–10; 10:11–18; 10:27–30.
122 Matthew 21:9
123 1 Samuel 17,34–5
124 Apocalypse 12:9
125 Ephesians 6: 14–15, 17
126 Ephesians 6:12
127 Luke 20:35–6
128 This text is based on John 15:1–8, the Gospel for the Fifth Sunday of Eastertide in the second year of the Lectionary cycle.
129 Psalm 80:8–11
130 *Didascalia Apostolorum: The Teaching of the Twelve Apostles*, 9
131 Deuteronomy 8:7
132 John 15:5
133 A reminiscence of St Augustine's Sermon 227, *Patrologia Latina* 38, 1099–1101.
134 Psalm 22:5 (Vulgate)
135 The prayer *Orate fratres* in the Mass of the Roman Rite
136 Ezekiel 15:2–3
137 Compare the Gospel readings for the Sixth Sunday of Eastertide in the first and third years of the Lectionary cycle: John 14:15–21; 14:23–9.
138 Philippians 2:1–4
139 Philippians 2:5
140 Hebrews 6:4–5
141 1 John 4:13
142 Acts of the Apostles 13:2
143 Ephesians 2:19–22
144 The Roman Lectionary permits the celebration of the Feast of the Ascension with its proper readings on the Seventh Sunday of Eastertide. See the Edizio Typica, I. 819.
145 Ignatius of Loyola, *Spiritual Exercises*, 344

146 Apocalypse 1:12
147 Luke 24:49
148 St Thomas Aquinas, *Summa Theologiae* IIa IIae, 188, 7c
149 From the prayer *Communicantes* in the Roman Canon
150 John 7:38–9
151 Exodus 31:3–5
152 Judges 6:34
153 Judges 14:6
154 Judges 15:14
155 Numbers 11:25
156 Micah 3:8
157 1 Samuel 16, 13
158 Wisdom of Solomon 1:7
159 T. S. Eliot, 'Little Gidding', *Four Quartets*, (Faber and Faber, London 1944)
160 Luke 23:34
161 Prayer of Absolution in the Roman Liturgy of Penance
162 St Jerome, *Dialogus contra Luciferianos 5, Patrologia Latina*, 23, 159A
163 1 John 5:3
164 Jonah 3:4
165 Mark 1:15
166 Exodus 3:14
167 Zechariah 14:9